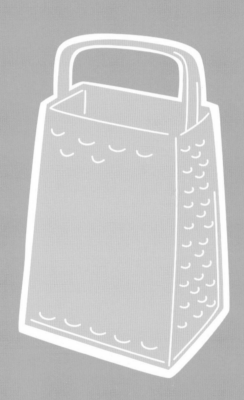

WILLIAMS-SONOMA

THE COOKBOOK
FOR KIDS

Great recipes for kids who love to cook

Photography **Erin Kunkel**

Text **Lisa Atwood**

weldon**owen**

Breakfast

8

Lunch

36

Snacks

66

Sweets

92

about this book

I learned to cook with a toy oven at the age of six. Soon enough, I was in the kitchen churning out enough muffins, cookies, and pies to start a bake shop, as well as Sunday morning omelets and after-school fruit smoothies.

Those early experiences nurtured a love of cooking I still have today. Through cooking, I found independence, a sense of accomplishment, and loads of adventure. Even now, those are still the parts of cooking I like the best.

Some of the recipes included here are inspired by the ones I used to make, and by what my own kids like to cook. You'll find a recipe for any time of the day and made with some of your favorite ingredients. So roll up your sleeves, pick a dish to cook, and get ready for a lifelong adventure!

Liz Atwood

Breakfast

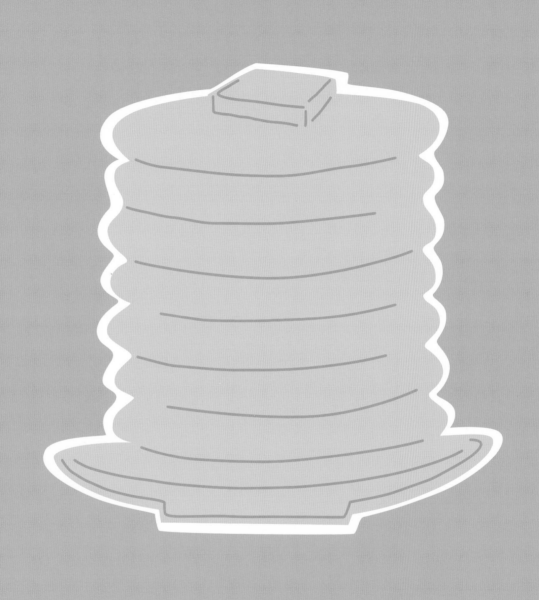

what you need

Large eggs 4

Milk ½ cup (4 fl oz/125 ml)

Vanilla extract ½ teaspoon

Store-bought or homemade cinnamon-swirl bread 4 thick slices (about 1 inch/2.5 cm each) (page 117)

Butter 1 tablespoon

popular toppings

Maple syrup, powdered sugar, fresh fruit

did you know?

Don't worry if your bread isn't super-fresh. French toast is best made with slightly stale bread, which won't fall apart when it's soaked with egg.

cinnamon-swirl french toast

1 first **soak the bread slices**

In a shallow bowl or baking dish, whisk together the eggs, milk, and vanilla. Add the bread slices and let soak, turning once or twice, until all of the egg mixture has been absorbed, about 10 minutes.

2 then **cook the french toast**

Heat a large frying pan or griddle over medium heat until hot, but not smoking. Add the butter. Using a spatula, spread the butter evenly over the pan bottom. Add the soaked bread slices in a single layer. Cook until the bottoms are golden, about 2 minutes. Slide the spatula underneath each bread slice and carefully flip it over. Cook until the second sides are golden and the centers puff slightly, about 2 minutes longer.

3 finally **serve the french toast**

Transfer the French toast to individual serving plates. Serve warm with your favorite toppings.

Makes 2–4 servings

easy french crepes

1 first melt the butter

Put the 2 tablespoons butter in a small microwave-safe bowl or cup and microwave on high (100%) power until melted, about 20 seconds.

2 then blend the ingredients

Pour the milk into a blender. Crack in the eggs, then pour in the melted butter. Add the flour, granulated sugar, baking powder, and salt. Blend briefly to mix. Using a rubber spatula, scrape down the sides of the blender. Blend again until smooth.

3 next cook the crepes

Place a 10-inch (25-cm) crepe pan or a nonstick frying pan over medium-high heat. When the pan is hot, spread a little bit of butter over the pan bottom with a spatula. Pour in about ⅓ cup (3 fl oz/80 ml) of the crepe batter all at once. Immediately tilt and swirl the pan so that the batter evenly covers the bottom. Cook the crepe until lightly browned on the bottom (you can lift an edge with the spatula to take a peek), about 2 minutes. Using the spatula, scoop under the center of the crepe and carefully flip it. While the second side is cooking, scoop a spoonful of your favorite filling onto the center of the crepe. When the second side is lightly browned, after about 2 minutes, slip the crepe, filling side up, onto a plate. Spread the filling evenly over the crepe, then fold it into quarters.

4 finally serve the crepes

Sprinkle the crepe with powdered sugar. Continue to cook the remaining crepes in the same way. Serve warm.

Makes 12 crepes; 4–6 servings

what you need

Butter 2 tablespoons, plus more for cooking the crepes

Milk 2 cups (16 fl oz/500 ml)

Large eggs 2

All-purpose flour 1½ cups (7½ oz/235 g)

Granulated sugar 1 tablespoon

Baking powder ½ teaspoon

Salt ½ teaspoon

Powdered sugar for dusting

popular fillings

Nutella, jam, strawberries and whipped cream, fresh fruit

did you know?

In Paris, street vendors make hot crepes to order with a selection of yummy fillings to choose from. Bon appétit!

what you need

Large egg 1

Low-fat buttermilk 2½ cups (20 fl oz/625 ml)

Butter 2 tablespoons, melted, plus more for cooking the pancakes and serving

All-purpose flour 1 cup (5 oz/155 g)

Sugar 1 tablespoon

Baking powder 1 teaspoon

Baking soda ½ teaspoon

Salt ½ teaspoon

Maple syrup for serving

did you know?

According to the 2001 Guinness Book of World Records, the largest pancake ever made weighed nearly 3 tons and was 49 feet, 3 inches (15 meters) in diameter!

buttermilk pancakes

1 first mix the ingredients

Crack the egg into a medium bowl and whisk until frothy. Add the buttermilk and melted butter and whisk gently just to combine. Add the flour, sugar, baking powder, baking soda, and salt and whisk gently just until the flour is incorporated.

2 then cook the pancakes

Heat a large frying pan or griddle over medium heat until hot, but not smoking. Add a little bit of butter to the pan and, using a spatula, spread it evenly over the bottom. For each pancake, spoon about ¼ cup (2 fl oz/60 ml) of the batter onto the pan, spacing them a few inches apart. Cook until the edges of the pancakes begin to look dry and the bottoms are golden brown, about 2 minutes. Slide a spatula underneath each pancake and carefully flip it over to cook the other side. Cook the pancakes on their second side until golden brown on the bottom and the batter is no longer runny in the center, about 1 minute longer. Continue to cook the remaining pancakes in the same way.

3 finally serve the pancakes

Using the spatula, slide the pancakes onto a serving plate. Serve warm with butter and syrup to drizzle over the top.

✳ variation banana pancakes

Use only 2 cups (16 fl oz/500 ml) buttermilk and add 1 mashed banana to the batter with the buttermilk. Cook as directed.

✳ variation chocolate chip pancakes

Just before cooking, stir ¼ cup (1½ oz/45 g) mini chocolate chips into the batter. Cook as directed.

Makes about 12 pancakes; 4 servings

cinnamon-sugar oatmeal

1 first cook the oatmeal

In a small saucepan over high heat, combine the milk, rolled oats, cinnamon, and a pinch of salt. Using a wooden spoon, stir until the mixture begins to simmer. Reduce the heat to medium and continue stirring until the oatmeal is thickened, about 4 minutes.

2 then serve the oatmeal

Divide the oatmeal between 2 bowls and top each serving with 1 tablespoon of the butter, if desired. Scatter each serving with half of the brown sugar and half of the chopped dried fruit. Serve hot.

✳ variations fresh fruit oatmeal

Instead of the dried fruit and brown sugar, top the oatmeal with 2 bananas, peeled and sliced, or ⅓ cup (1½ oz/45 g) blueberries, and a drizzle of heavy cream.

Makes 2 servings

what you need

Milk 2 cups (16 fl oz/500 ml)

Rolled oats 1 cup (3 oz/90 g)

Cinnamon ½ teaspoon

Salt

Butter 2 tablespoons (optional)

Golden brown sugar
1 tablespoon firmly packed

Dried fruit such as apricots, figs, peaches, pitted dates, apples, or raisins about 1 cup (6 oz/185 g) chopped

did you know?

Dried fruit is regular fruit that has been dehydrated to remove the fruit's natural moisture. This makes the fruit last longer and gives it a nice, chewy texture and concentrated flavor.

what you need

Butter 6 tablespoons
(3 oz/90 g), cut into pieces

All-purpose flour 2 cups
(10 oz/315 g)

Sugar 1 tablespoon

Baking powder 1 tablespoon

Salt ¼ teaspoon

Large eggs 3

Milk 1½ cups (12 fl oz/375 ml)

popular toppings

Maple syrup, jam, fresh berries, whipped cream

did you know?

The key to light, crisp waffles is to beat the eggs until they are very frothy and pale. Use a wire whisk or, to make it easier, an electric mixer.

waffles with toppings

1 **first melt the butter**

Put the butter in a small microwave-safe bowl or cup and microwave on high (100%) power until melted, about 25 seconds. Preheat a waffle iron.

2 **then mix the batter**

In a medium bowl, whisk together the flour, sugar, baking powder, and salt. In a large bowl, beat the eggs until light and frothy (see note). Add the milk and melted butter. Using a whisk or large spoon, gradually stir in the flour mixture just until incorporated. (The batter will be lumpy.)

3 **finally cook the waffles and serve**

Pour some batter over the cooking grid of the waffle iron until it's two-thirds covered. Close the lid and cook until the steam subsides or the indicator light signals that the waffle is ready, 1–3 minutes. Carefully open the iron and transfer the waffle to a serving plate. Continue to cook the remaining waffles in the same way. Serve warm with your favorite toppings.

* **variation nut and seed waffles**

Just before cooking the batter, stir in 3 tablespoons lightly toasted, chopped pecans and 3 tablespoons lightly toasted raw sunflower seeds.

Makes about 8 waffles; 4–6 servings

what you need

Butter 6 tablespoons (3 oz/90 g)

Large eggs 4

Milk 1 cup (8 fl oz/250 ml)

All-purpose flour 1 cup
(5 oz/155 g)

Blackberries ½ cup (2 oz/60 g)

Powdered sugar for dusting

did you know?

The original "Dutch baby"
oven-baked pancakes were
derived from a recipe for large
German pancakes served in a
family-run Seattle restaurant in
the early 1900s. Traditional ones
rise dramatically at the sides
during baking, while these
miniature versions puff
just as nicely in
the middle.

dutch baby pancakes

1 ### first **heat the pans**

Preheat the oven to 400°F (200°C). Have ready six 10-oz
(315-g) ramekins or four 5-inch (13-cm) pie tins. Divide the
butter evenly among the dishes. Place the dishes in the oven.

2 ### then **mix the ingredients**

While the butter is melting, crack the eggs into a blender.
Blend on low speed for 1 minute. With the motor running,
gradually pour in the milk, then the flour. Blend until smooth.

3 ### next **bake the batter**

Wearing oven mitts, remove the dishes from the oven
and, using a pastry brush, lightly brush the butter over
the bottom and up the sides of each dish. Carefully pour
an equal amount of the batter into each dish. Add the
berries, dividing them evenly between the dishes. Bake
until puffed and golden, 17–19 minutes.

4 ### finally **serve the pancakes**

When the pancakes are ready, remove the dishes from
the oven, transfer to serving plates, and serve at once
while they are still nice and puffy and warm. Dust with
powdered sugar as desired.

Makes 4–6 servings

bacon & spinach frittata

1 first thaw the spinach

Let the package of spinach thaw, then separate out about one-fourth of the leaves. Reserve the remaining spinach for another use. Rinse the spinach in your hands over the sink and squeeze out any excess water.

2 then cook the bacon and onion

Heat an 8-inch (20-cm) nonstick ovenproof frying pan over medium heat. Add the bacon and cook, stirring often, until lightly browned on the edges, 3–4 minutes. Remove the pan from the heat. Using a slotted spoon, transfer the bacon to a paper towel–lined plate. Place the pan over low heat and add the onion. Cook, stirring, for about 2 minutes. Add the onion to the plate with the bacon and set aside. Reserve the pan.

3 next combine the ingredients

Preheat the oven to 375°F (190°C). Crack the eggs into a large bowl. Add the cream and whisk until blended. Add the cheese, spinach, bacon, and onion. Stir gently until mixed.

4 finally cook the frittata and serve

Pour the egg mixture into the reserved pan. Return to low heat and cook, using the spatula to lift the cooked edges and allow the uncooked egg to run underneath, until there is no more runny egg, 3–4 minutes. Place the pan in the oven and bake until the eggs are puffy and set, 8–10 minutes. Let the frittata cool for a few minutes. Asking an adult for help and using oven mitts, hold a serving plate upside down over the pan and turn the pan and plate together, releasing the frittata onto the plate. Cut into squares or wedges to serve. Serve warm or at room temperature.

Makes 4–6 servings

what you need

Frozen spinach leaves
¼ package (2½ oz/75 g)

Bacon, 4 strips, thinly sliced crosswise

Green onion 2 tablespoons finely chopped

Large eggs 8

Heavy cream 2 tablespoons

Monterey Jack cheese ¾ cup (3 oz/90 g) shredded

did you know?

Frittata was first served in Italy and comes from the Italian word "fritto," which means "fried."

chicken-apple sausage & cheese scramble

1 first brown the sausage

In a large nonstick pan over medium heat, cook the sausage, turning often, until evenly browned, about 5 minutes. Transfer the sausage to a cutting board and let cool, then cut crosswise into thin slices.

2 then whisk the eggs

Crack the eggs into a large bowl. Add 1 tablespoon water and whisk just until the whites and yolks are blended.

3 next scramble the ingredients

Heat a 12-inch (30-cm) nonstick frying pan over low heat. When the pan is warm, add the butter, carefully tilting and swirling the pan to spread the butter evenly over the pan bottom. Add the onion and cook, stirring almost constantly, until tender, 2–3 minutes. Stir in the sausage slices. Raise the heat to medium and, when the pan begins to get hotter but the onions have not yet begun to brown, add the eggs. Cook, using the spatula to scrape the cooked eggs from the bottom of the pan and allow the uncooked egg to run underneath, until the eggs are creamy, about 4 minutes. Add the cheese and stir gently until melted, about 2 minutes.

4 finally serve the scramble

Remove the pan from the heat and divide the scrambled eggs among 4 serving plates. Serve hot. Let everyone season their own portion with salt and pepper as desired.

Makes 4 servings

what you need

Fully-cooked chicken-apple sausage 1

Large eggs 6

Butter 1 tablespoon

Green onion 1 tablespoon finely chopped

Monterey Jack or Cheddar cheese ⅓ cup (1½ oz/45 g) shredded and firmly packed

Salt and freshly ground pepper

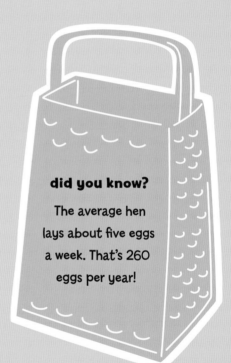

did you know?

The average hen lays about five eggs a week. That's 260 eggs per year!

what you need

Sandwich bread 4 slices

Butter 2 tablespoons, plus more for cooking the eggs

Large eggs 4

Salt and freshly ground pepper

did you know?

"Eggs in a hole" has lots of different names, depending on who you talk to. It also goes by "eggs in a basket," "bird's nest," "frog in the hole," or "toad in the hole."

eggs in a hole

1 first cut the holes

Spread both sides of the bread evenly with the butter. Using a 3-inch (7.5-cm) round cutter, cut a circle out of the center of each piece of bread and set aside.

2 then cook the eggs and bread

Heat a 12-inch (30-cm) nonstick frying pan or griddle over medium heat until hot, but not smoking. Add a little bit of butter, carefully tilting and swirling the pan to spread the butter evenly over the pan bottom. When the pan is hot and the butter is melted, place the bread, including the cutout circles, in a single, even layer in the pan. Crack an egg into the hole in each slice of bread and sprinkle lightly with salt and pepper. Let the egg cook until it just begins to turn opaque, 2–3 minutes. Slide a spatula under each slice of bread and its egg and carefully turn them over together. Continue to cook until the yolk is still runny but the white is cooked through, about 30 seconds more. Turn the cutout circles as well, cooking them until nicely browned on both sides.

3 finally serve the eggs

Using the spatula, slide each egg in a hole onto a serving plate with a "hole" alongside it. Serve hot.

Makes 4 servings

the perfect omelet

1 first **beat the eggs**

Crack the eggs into a bowl. Season with salt and pepper and add 1 teaspoon water. Whisk the eggs just until the whites and yolks are blended.

2 then **cook the eggs**

Place a 7-inch (18-cm) nonstick omelet pan over medium-high heat. When the pan is hot, add the butter, carefully tilting and swirling the pan to spread the butter evenly over the pan bottom. When the foam subsides, add the eggs and let cook for a few seconds. Using a spatula, push one side of the omelet toward the center of the pan, tilting the pan gently so the uncooked egg runs under the cooked egg and over the exposed pan bottom. Continue along the other sides of the pan until there is no more runny egg. The top should still be creamy. Add a couple spoonfuls of your favorite fillings over the top of the omelet.

3 finally **serve the omelet**

Holding the omelet pan by the handle over a serving plate, slide the omelet onto the plate. Let the omelet cool slightly. Then, using your fingertips or a fork and knife, roll it up to conceal the filling inside. Serve hot.

Makes 1 serving

what you need

Large eggs 2
Salt and freshly ground pepper
Butter 1 teaspoon

popular fillings

Shredded cheese, ham, cooked bacon, avocado, bell peppers, onions, and tomatoes

did you know?

Adding just a teaspoon of water to beaten eggs before cooking gives them a slightly lighter and more airy texture than plain cooked eggs. The water creates steam, which forces air through the eggs, making them fluffier.

what you need

Vanilla yogurt 1 container (about 6 oz/185 g)

Mixed berries, such as blueberries, blackberries, and raspberries ⅓ cup (1½ oz/45 g)

Granola 2 tablespoons

did you know?

The traditional tall parfait glass is perfect for seeing the layers of fruit and yogurt in this light treat. If you don't have one, your favorite dessert bowl will also do.

berry & yogurt parfaits

1 first layer the parfait

Spoon the yogurt into the bottom of an individual bowl or parfait glass. Spoon the berries in an even layer onto the yogurt. Spoon the granola over the top.

2 then serve the parfait

Serve cold with a spoon for digging down through the layers.

✳ variation kiwi and yogurt parfaits

Instead of berries, use 1 kiwi, peeled and sliced or diced.

Makes 1 parfait

broiled grapefruit halves

what you need

Grapefruits 3

Golden brown sugar
6 tablespoons (2½ oz/75 g)
firmly packed

1 first **cut the grapefruit**

Preheat the broiler. Line a baking sheet with aluminum foil. Cut the grapefruits in half crosswise and use a small serrated knife to loosen or separate the segments.

2 then **broil the grapefruit**

Arrange the grapefruit halves, cut sides up, on the prepared sheet. Sprinkle each half with 1 tablespoon of the brown sugar. Have an adult help you place the grapefruit halves in the broiler about 4 inches (10 cm) from the heat source. Broil until the sugar has melted and is bubbling, 2–3 minutes.

3 finally **serve the grapefruit**

Transfer the grapefruit halves to individual bowls and serve at once with a grapefruit spoon, if desired.

Makes 6 servings

did you know?

Grapefruits look and taste very different from grapes, but they share the same name. Why? Because grapefruits grow in bunches—the same way grapes do!

what you need

Butter ½ cup (4 oz/125 g), melted, plus more for greasing the pan

All-purpose flour 2¼ cups (11½ oz/360 g), plus more for dusting the pan

Sugar 1 cup (8 oz/250 g)

Baking soda 1 teaspoon

Salt ½ teaspoon

Very ripe bananas 3

Large eggs 2, lightly beaten

Plain yogurt ⅓ cup (3 oz/90 g)

Vanilla extract 1 teaspoon

Walnuts 1 cup (4 oz/125 g) chopped (optional)

the best banana bread

1 first mix the ingredients

Preheat the oven to 350°F (180°C). Butter and flour a 5-by-9-inch (13-by-23-cm) loaf pan. In a medium bowl, mix together the flour, sugar, baking soda, and salt. In a large bowl, mash the bananas well with a fork. Add the butter, eggs, yogurt, and vanilla. Stir until blended. Gradually add the flour mixture, stirring gently just until mixed. Stir in the nuts, if using. Scrape the batter into the prepared loaf pan.

2 then bake the bread

Bake until a toothpick inserted into the center comes out clean, about 1 hour. If the top begins to brown too much during baking, cover loosely with aluminum foil. Let the pan cool on a wire rack for 10 minutes, then turn the bread out on the rack, turn right side up, and let cool completely.

3 finally serve the bread

Cut the bread into slices and serve at room temperature.

Makes 8–10 servings

did you know?

You're better off using really ripe, even brown-speckled bananas for this big loaf. The riper the bananas, the more flavorful and moist the bread will be.

monkey bread

1 **first prepare the pan and toppings**

Using a pastry brush, brush the inside of a 10-inch (25-cm) Bundt pan with some of the melted butter. Set aside the remaining butter in a shallow bowl. In another shallow bowl, mix together the brown sugar, ½ cup pecans, and cinnamon and set aside. Sprinkle the remaining 2 tablespoons pecans over the bottom of the pan.

2 **then assemble the loaf**

Place the homemade dough or the thawed rolls on a lightly floured work surface. If using homemade dough, cut it into golf ball–size pieces. Working with a few rolls or pieces of dough at a time, roll the dough in the melted butter and then turn to coat in the brown-sugar mixture. Place the coated dough pieces in a roughly even layer in the prepared pan.

3 **next let it rise**

Preheat the oven to 350°F (180°C) for 5 minutes, then turn off the oven. Cover the pan loosely with aluminum foil and place in the warm oven. Let the dough rise until doubled in bulk, about 1 hour. Remove the pan from the oven and preheat the oven to 375°F (190°C).

4 **finally bake the bread**

Bake until richly browned and a toothpick inserted into the center of the loaf comes out clean, 20–25 minutes for the homemade dough or 30–35 minutes for the store-bought rolls. Remove the pan from the oven and set on a wire rack to cool for 5 minutes. Using oven mitts, hold a serving plate upside down over the pan, then turn the pan and plate together, releasing the loaf onto the plate. Serve warm.

Makes 10–12 servings

what you need

Butter ½ cup (4 oz/125 g), melted

Golden brown sugar 1 cup (7 oz/220 g) firmly packed

Pecans ½ cup (2 oz/60 g) plus 2 tablespoons finely chopped

Ground cinnamon 2½ teaspoons

Sweet White Bread dough (page 116) or store-bought frozen Parker House–style rolls 1 package (25 oz/780 g) thawed

All-purpose flour for dusting

did you know?

The origin of the name "monkey bread" is uncertain. One theory is, since most kids like to enjoy it ball by sticky ball, it evokes what your moms might call "eating like a monkey."

mini blueberry muffins

1 first mix the wet ingredients

Preheat the oven to 400°F (200°C). Grease a 24-cup mini muffin pan. In a large glass measuring pitcher, whisk together the eggs, brown sugar, oil, cream, milk, and vanilla.

2 then add the dry ingredients

In a large bowl, sift together the flour, baking powder, nutmeg, and salt. Make a well in the center and slowly pour in the egg mixture. Gradually stir into the dry ingredients until just combined. Add the melted butter and stir until almost smooth but still slightly lumpy. Do not overmix. The batter will be fairly thick. Gently fold the blueberries into the batter so that they are evenly distributed.

3 finally bake the muffins

Spoon the batter into the muffin cups, filling each about three-fourths full. Bake until a toothpick inserted into the center of a muffin comes out clean, 12–14 minutes. Let stand in the pan for 5 minutes, then use a spatula to remove each mini muffin. Serve warm.

Makes 24 mini muffins

what you need

Large eggs 2

Golden brown sugar ½ cup (3½ oz/105 g) firmly packed

Canola oil ⅓ cup (3 fl oz/80 ml)

Heavy cream ½ cup (4 fl oz/125 ml)

Milk ½ cup (4 fl oz/125 ml)

Vanilla extract 1½ teaspoons

All-purpose flour 2¼ cups (11½ oz/360 g)

Baking powder 2 teaspoons

Ground nutmeg ¼ teaspoon

Salt ⅛ teaspoon

Butter 3 tablespoons, melted

Blueberries 1½ cups (6 oz/185 g)

did you know?

Blueberries are considered a "super food" because they are incredibly high in antioxidants, which help us fight diseases and stay healthy.

what you need

for the streusel topping

Golden brown sugar
3 tablespoons firmly packed

All-purpose flour 2 tablespoons

Ground nutmeg and ground cinnamon ¼ teaspoon *each*

Walnuts ¼ cup (1 oz/30 g) chopped

Butter 1 tablespoon, at room temperature

for the muffins

All-purpose flour 1½ cups (7½ oz/235 g)

Baking soda 1 teaspoon

Baking powder ½ teaspoon

Salt ½ teaspoon

Ground cinnamon, cloves, and nutmeg ½ teaspoon *each*

Canned pumpkin purée 1 cup (8 oz/250 g)

Granulated sugar 1½ cups (12 oz/375 g)

Canola oil ½ cup (4 fl oz/125 ml)

Large eggs 2, at room temperature, lightly beaten

Vanilla extract ½ teaspoon

did you know?

The largest pumpkin ever recorded weighed in at 1,725 lb (782 kg) at a pumpkin festival in Ohio.

pumpkin muffins

1 first **make the topping**

In a small bowl, stir together the brown sugar, flour, nutmeg, and cinnamon. Add in the nuts and mix well. Add the butter and, using your fingertips, rub it into the nut mixture until blended. Set aside.

2 then **mix the ingredients**

Preheat the oven to 350°F (180°C). Line a 12-cup muffin pan with paper liners. In a bowl, stir together the flour, baking soda, baking powder, salt, cinnamon, cloves, and nutmeg. Set aside. In a large bowl, combine the pumpkin, granulated sugar, oil, eggs, and vanilla and stir until well mixed. Stir in the flour mixture just until blended.

3 finally **bake the muffins**

Divide the batter evenly between the muffin cups. Sprinkle the topping evenly over the tops. Bake until a toothpick inserted into the center of a muffin comes out clean, about 20 minutes. Let cool in the pan on a wire rack for 5 minutes. Tilt the pan to release the muffin, set them upright on the rack, and let cool completely. Serve at room temperature.

Makes 12 muffins

smoothie bar

monday **mango-banana**

Start the week with this healthy favorite. Mangoes are loaded with vitamin C and bananas have energy-boosting potassium. Look for frozen mango cubes in the freezer section of your market.

tuesday **piña colada**

This creamy smoothie combines pineapple and coconut cream, which is sold in a can, in an alcohol-free rendition of a popular tropical cocktail. To make it extra-special, serve it in a hollowed-out coconut or pineapple.

wednesday **strawberry-guava**

Guava nectar is the key to the satisfying sweetness of this pink-hued treat. For a special garnish, cut a small slit in the bottom of a fresh strawberry and nestle it onto the rim of your glass before serving.

thursday **very berry**

Take one sip of this berry smoothie and your mouth will go zing! If you prefer a mellower flavor, add a few tablespoons of cream or milk, or a spoonful of yogurt, and whirl until blended.

friday **creamy peach**

Pineapple juice and banana bring a hint of the tropics to the sweet flavor of this summer fruit. A scoop of vanilla yogurt adds a cool creaminess. Garnish each glass with a slice of fresh peach or pineapple, if you like.

Makes 2 servings each

what you need

Fruit smoothies are easy to make. Just put a few ice cubes and the listed ingredients in a blender and process for 1–2 minutes, or until smooth, adding more juice or ice as needed to create the consistency you like. To layer a smoothie, fill a glass half full with one flavor, then pour a second flavor over the back of a spoon to create a top layer. Serve cold.

mango-banana
Banana 1
Frozen mango cubes 2 cups (12 oz/375 g)
Vanilla yogurt ½ cup (4 oz/125 g)
Orange juice 1 cup (8 fl oz/250 ml)

piña colada
Bananas 1½
Frozen pineapple cubes 1 cup (6 oz/185 g)
Milk ½ cup (4 fl oz/125 ml)
Coconut cream 1½ tablespoons
Pineapple juice ½ cup
(4 fl oz/125 ml)

strawberry-guava
Frozen strawberries 2 cups (8 oz/250 g)
Vanilla yogurt ½ cup (4 oz/125 g)
Guava nectar ½ cup (4 fl oz/125 ml)

very berry
Frozen blueberries 1 cup (4 oz/125 g)
Frozen strawberries 1 cup (4 oz/125 g)
Raspberry sorbet ½ cup (4 oz/125 g)
Vanilla yogurt ½ cup (4 oz/125 g)
Cranraspberry juice 1 cup
(8 fl oz/250 ml)

creamy peach
Frozen peach slices 2 cups (12 oz/375 g)
Small banana 1
Vanilla yogurt ½ cup (4 oz/125 g)
Pineapple juice ½ cup (4 fl oz/125 ml)

Lunch

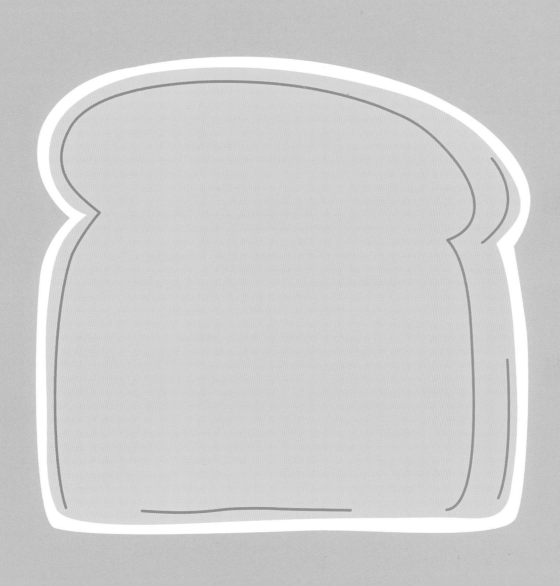

what you need

Olive oil 1 tablespoon

Yellow onion ¾ cup (3 oz/90 g) chopped

Garlic cloves 2, minced

Kale 2 stalks, well rinsed, stems removed, and leaves coarsely chopped

Low-sodium chicken or vegetable broth 6 cups (48 fl oz/1.5 l)

Diced tomatoes 1 can (14½ oz/455 g)

Frozen vegetable medley such as green beans, carrots, peas, and corn 1½ cups (about 8 oz/250 g)

Cauliflower florets 1 cup (2 oz/60 g) bite-size

Salt and freshly ground pepper

Small pasta ½ cup (2 oz/60 g)

Cannellini beans ¾ cup (5 oz/155 g)

Store-bought pesto about ¼ cup (2½ oz/75 g) (optional)

did you know?

"Minestra" is the Italian word for "soup," and minestrone is by far Italy's most popular variety.

minestrone soup

1 first **cook the vegetables**

In a soup pot, heat the oil over medium-low heat. Add the onion and cook, stirring often, until tender, 7–10 minutes. (While the onions are cooking, bring a pot of water to a boil for cooking the pasta.) Add the garlic to the pot and cook, stirring often, for 1 minute longer. Add the kale and cook, stirring often, until it begins to wilt, about 1 minute. Add the broth, the tomatoes and their juices, the frozen vegetables, and the cauliflower. Bring just to a boil over high heat, then reduce the heat to medium-low and simmer until the vegetables are tender but still crisp, about 5 minutes.

2 then **add the pasta and beans**

When the pot of water comes to a boil, add ¼ teaspoon salt and then the pasta. Boil the pasta until firm but tender to the bite, about 7 minutes or according to the package directions. Drain the pasta in a colander set in the sink. Add the drained pasta to the soup. Rinse and drain the beans in the colander, then add to the soup. Simmer until the beans are heated through, about 5 minutes longer. Season with salt and pepper.

3 finally **serve the soup**

Ladle the soup into warmed individual bowls. Add a generous spoonful of pesto, if using, to each bowl just before serving. Serve hot. Store any leftover soup in a covered container in the refrigerator up to 5 days, or freeze for up to 6 months.

Makes 6–8 servings

creamy tomato soup

1 first make the soup

In a large saucepan over medium heat, warm the oil and butter. When the butter is melted, add the onion and cook, stirring often, until tender and translucent, 5–7 minutes. Add the garlic and cook, stirring frequently, for 2 minutes longer. Add the tomatoes and their juices and the broth. Bring to a boil over high heat. Reduce the heat to medium-low and simmer, stirring occasionally, for 20 minutes.

2 then purée the soup

Remove the saucepan from the heat and let the tomato mixture cool slightly. You can purée the soup using an immersion blender or a regular blender. To use an immersion blender, submerge the end of the blender stick in the soup and carefully purée until smooth. To use a regular blender, let the soup cool until lukewarm. Working in batches, transfer the soup to the blender and purée until smooth. Pour each batch into a large bowl until all of the soup is puréed, then return all of the soup to the saucepan.

3 finally add the cream and seasonings

Return the saucepan to medium-low heat and stir in the cream. Add the salt and pepper. Heat, stirring, until steaming. Serve hot.

Makes 6 servings

what you need

Olive oil 1 tablespoon

Butter 2 tablespoons

Yellow onion 1, coarsely chopped

Garlic cloves 2, minced

Diced tomatoes 1 can (28 oz/875 g)

Low-sodium chicken or vegetable broth 4 cups (32 fl oz/1 l)

Heavy cream ½ cup (4 fl oz/125 ml)

Salt and freshly ground pepper ½ teaspoon *each* or to taste

did you know?

For a fun presentation, serve this soup in bread bowls made from hollowed-out small, round sourdough loaves. Or, pair with Big Cheese Twists (page 68) or Ham & Cheese Panini (page 48).

what you need

Olive oil 1 tablespoon

Yellow onion ¾ cup (3 oz/90 g) chopped

Ground beef 1½ lb (750 g)

Garlic cloves 4, minced

Chili powder 2 tablespoons plus 2 teaspoons

Ground cumin 1½ teaspoons

Dried basil ½ teaspoon

Dried oregano ½ teaspoon

Low-sodium chicken broth 2 cups (16 fl oz/500 ml)

Crushed tomatoes 1 can (14 oz/440 g)

Tomato paste ¼ cup (2 oz/60 g)

Chili beans in sauce 1 can (15½ oz/485 g)

Salt and freshly ground pepper

Cheddar cheese ½ cup (2 oz/60 g) shredded

chili with cheese

1 first brown the beef

In a large, heavy pot over medium heat, warm the oil. Add the onion and cook, stirring often, until translucent, about 5 minutes. Add the ground beef and garlic and cook, using a wooden spoon to break the meat up into small pieces, until the beef is browned, 5–7 minutes.

2 then add the spices and tomatoes

Add the chili powder, cumin, basil, and oregano. Stir to mix well. Stir in the chicken broth, crushed tomatoes and their juices, and tomato paste. Reduce the heat to medium-low and simmer, stirring occasionally, until the mixture has a thick and chunky consistency, about 1 hour.

3 finally serve the chili

Stir in the beans and simmer for 5 minutes longer. Season with salt and pepper. Spoon the chili into individual bowls and sprinkle the cheese evenly over the tops. Serve hot.

Makes 4–5 servings

did you know?

If you like your chili extra-spicy, use a heavy hand when adding the chili powder.

teriyaki chicken bowls

1 first cook the rice

Cook the rice according to the package directions. Remove from the heat and set aside, covered.

2 then prepare and grill the chicken

Heat a grill pan over medium-high heat until hot. Place the chicken on a plate. Drizzle the oil over the chicken and turn to evenly coat. Season with salt and pepper. Pour ½ cup (4 fl oz/125 ml) of the teriyaki sauce into a shallow bowl to use for brushing. Place the chicken, cut side up, on the grill pan. Grill until the edges turn opaque and dark brown grill marks appear on the bottom, 3–5 minutes. Using tongs, turn the chicken. Using a basting brush, brush the chicken with plenty of teriyaki sauce. Grill until dark brown grill marks appear on the second sides and the chicken is opaque when cut into with a knife, about 2 minutes longer. Using the tongs, transfer the chicken to a cutting board. Heat the remaining ½ cup (4 fl oz/125 ml) teriyaki sauce in a small saucepan over low heat, stirring occasionally, until hot, about 5 minutes.

3 next cook the vegetables

Meanwhile, bring a pot of water to a boil over high heat. Add the broccoli, asparagus, and carrot and cook for 1 minute. Drain and rinse under cold running water.

4 finally assemble the bowls

Divide the rice equally among 4 bowls. Cut the chicken pieces on the diagonal into slices and arrange over the rice. Divide the vegetables, the sauce, and the sesame seeds, if using, among the bowls. Serve hot.

Makes 4 servings

what you need

Long-grain white rice 1 cup (7 oz/220 g)

Skinless, boneless chicken breast 1 large (about 6 oz/185 g), cut into 2 thin halves (keeping the knife parallel to the cutting board)

Olive oil 1 teaspoon

Salt and freshly ground pepper

Store-bought teriyaki sauce or glaze 1 cup (8 fl oz/250 ml)

Broccoli florets 2 cups (about 4 oz/125 g)

Asparagus spears 4, woody ends removed, cut on the diagonal into 1-inch (2.5-cm) pieces

Large carrot 1, peeled and sliced on the diagonal (about 1 cup)

Toasted sesame seeds 1 tablespoon (optional)

did you know?

The term "teriyaki" is a combination of two Japanese words: "teri," which means shine or luster, and "yaki," which refers to grilling or broiling.

chinese chicken salad

1 first cook the chicken

Put the chicken in a small saucepan or sauté pan in a single layer. Pour in just enough broth to cover the chicken. Cover the pan and bring to a boil over high heat. Reduce the heat to low and simmer until the chicken is opaque throughout when cut into with a knife, 10–15 minutes. Using tongs, transfer the chicken to a plate and let cool. Discard the broth. When cool enough to handle, shred the chicken into bite-size pieces.

2 then combine the ingredients

In a salad bowl, combine the salad greens, cucumber, snow peas, and bean sprouts and toss gently with tongs. Scatter the chicken evenly over the top, then sprinkle with the almonds and the orange slices, if using.

3 finally toss with the dressing

Drizzle the dressing over the salad. Using the tongs or a large fork and spoon, gently toss the salad until evenly coated with the dressing. Divide the salad evenly among 4 salad plates. Sprinkle each serving with the rice noodles, if using, then serve.

Makes 4 servings

what you need

Skinless, boneless chicken breast halves 2 small (about 8 oz/250 g)

Low-sodium chicken broth about 2 cups (16 fl oz/500 ml)

Mixed baby greens or shredded lettuce 4 cups (4 oz/125 g)

English cucumber ½, peeled, halved lengthwise, and sliced

Snow peas 1 cup (about 5 oz/155 g), trimmed

Bean sprouts 1 cup (about 2 oz/60 g)

Toasted sliced almonds 1 tablespoon

Canned mandarin orange slices ⅓ cup (1½ oz/40 g), drained (optional)

Store-bought or homemade Asian dressing (see note) ½ cup (4 fl oz/125 ml)

Fried rice noodles about ¼ cup (1 oz/30 g) (optional)

did you know?

For a great homemade Asian dressing, mix together 2 tablespoons teriyaki sauce, 1 tablespoon each safflower oil, mayonnaise, and rice vinegar, and 1 teaspoon each sesame oil and peeled, grated fresh ginger. Yum!

what you need

Flatbreads (see note) 4

Chopped romaine lettuce 1 cup
(1 oz/30 g)

English cucumber ¼, peeled
and chopped

Plum tomato 1, chopped

Kalamata olives 2 tablespoons
chopped

Crumbled feta cheese
2 tablespoons

Small red onion ¼, thinly sliced

Olive oil 1½ tablespoons

Red wine vinegar 2 teaspoons

**Tsatsiki (page 119) or
store-bought hummus** ¼ cup
(2 oz/60 g)

**Cooked chopped or shredded
chicken (page 44)**
¼ lb (250 g), heated (optional)

did you know?

Lots of different types
of flatbread work well in this
recipe. Try regular or whole-
wheat pita pocket breads, halved,
split, and stuffed rather than
used whole, or rounds
of Indian naan
or chapati.

greek salad wraps

1 **first heat the breads**

Preheat the oven to 400°F (200°C). Wrap the breads in
aluminum foil and place in the oven to warm for 5 minutes.

2 **then make the salad**

Meanwhile, in a bowl, combine the lettuce, cucumber,
tomato, olives, cheese, and onion. In a small bowl or glass,
using a fork, stir together the oil and vinegar to make a
dressing. Drizzle the dressing over the top of the salad.
Using tongs or 2 large spoons, toss the salad until well mixed.

3 **finally wrap it up**

Place four 10-inch (25-cm) squares of aluminum foil on a
work surface. Unwrap the breads and place each one on
a foil square. Spread each bread with 1 tablespoon of the
tsatsiki or hummus and sprinkle the salad in a thick layer
on top, diving it evenly. Scatter the meat, if using, over the
salad, again dividing evenly. Starting at one side, roll each
wrap, using the foil to hold it together snugly. Serve warm.

Makes 4 wraps

what you need

Olive oil 1 tablespoon, if needed

Ground beef or turkey
1¼ lb (625 g)

Golden brown sugar
2 tablespoons firmly packed

Dried minced onion
2 tablespoons

Paprika 1 teaspoon

Chili powder 1 teaspoon

Garlic powder ½ teaspoon

Tomato sauce 1 can (15 fl oz/465 ml)

Tomato paste 2 tablespoons

Worcestershire sauce
2 tablespoons

Red wine vinegar 2 teaspoons

Salt and freshly ground pepper

Hamburger buns 4, split

did you know?

It's easy to understand why it's
called "sloppy," but why "Joe"?
Turns out, the original Sloppy Joe
was named not for its messiness,
but for Sloppy Joe's bar in
Key West, Florida, where the
meaty dish was invented.

sloppy joes

1 first cook the filling

Place a large frying pan over medium-high heat. If you are
using turkey, add the oil to the skillet to keep it from sticking.
Add the meat and cook, using a wooden spoon to break it up
into small pieces, until evenly cooked, 8–10 minutes. (Ask an
adult to help you pour off the fat if the mixture seems too
greasy.) Reduce the heat to medium-low and add the brown
sugar, onion, paprika, chili powder, and garlic powder. Cook,
stirring, until blended, about 2 minutes.

2 then add flavor

Add the tomato sauce, tomato paste, Worcestershire sauce,
and vinegar. Stir until well mixed. Bring to a boil over high
heat. Immediately reduce the heat to medium-low and cook,
stirring often to blend the flavors, about 5 minutes longer.
Season to taste with salt and pepper.

3 finally serve the joes

Place a bun bottom, cut side up, on each of 4 plates. Spoon
an equal amount of the meat mixture over the buns, then
place the bun tops on top. Serve hot.

Makes 4 servings

ham & cheese panini

1 first **build the panini**

Top each of 2 of the bread slices with 2 slices of cheese, half of the ham, and another 2 slices of cheese. Then, top each sandwich with one of the remaining bread slices. Spread 1 tablespoon of butter over the top of each sandwich, and then 1 tablespoon on the bottom of each.

2 then **cook the panini**

If using a panini press, preheat it to 400°F (200°C). If using a frying pan, heat a 12-inch (30-cm) nonstick frying pan over medium heat. Carefully place the panini in the press, lower the lid, and cook until golden brown on both sides, 4–5 minutes. If using a frying pan, cook, turning once, until golden brown on both sides, 2–3 minutes per side. Use a spatula to gently press down on the panini once or twice while each side cooks.

3 finally **serve the panini**

Using the spatula, transfer the panini to a cutting board. When they are cool enough to handle, cut the panini diagonally in half. Serve 1 warm panini half per person.

✳ variation **pesto panini**

Add 1 tablespoon store-bought pesto to each sandwich, spreading it on the inside of one of the bread slices before adding the cheese.

✳ variation **tomato panini**

Core and finely chop 1 plum tomato and divide between the sandwiches, spreading the tomatoes over the first layer of cheese before adding the ham.

Makes 2 large panini; 4 servings

what you need

Sourdough bread 4 large slices, each about 8 inches (20 cm) wide

Provolone, Monterey Jack, or Swiss cheese, 8 slices (about 10 oz/315 g)

Ham ½ lb (250 g), sliced

Butter, 4 tablespoons (2 oz/60 g), at room temperature

did you know?

"Panini" is an Italian word for "sandwiches." An electric panini press is a grill that cooks both sides of a sandwich at the same time, but a frying pan works well, too.

what you need

Soft French rolls 4

Soy sauce ⅓ cup (3 fl oz/80 ml)

Rosemary 1 teaspoon chopped fresh, or ½ teaspoon dried

Thyme 1 teaspoon chopped fresh, or ½ teaspoon dried

Large garlic clove 1, minced

Thinly sliced cooked roast beef 1 lb (500 g)

Beef bouillon cubes 2

did you know?

Is the French dip really French? Well, it's served on a French roll, and it was first served at Philippe's, a French restaurant in Los Angeles (in 1908!), but that's where the French connection comes to an end. Few people in France know about this popular dish.

french dip

1 first **prepare the rolls**

Preheat the broiler. Slice the sandwich rolls lengthwise in half. (Cut a slice out of the middle to make the roll a bit thinner if it looks too big for your mouth.) Place the rolls, cut side up, on a baking sheet and broil until lightly browned. (Ask an adult to help you broil the rolls, if you like.) Turn off the oven. Wrap the toasted rolls in aluminum foil and place in the oven to keep warm while you prepare the roast beef.

2 then **flavor the beef**

In a small saucepan, stir together 1½ cups (12 fl oz/375 ml) water, the soy sauce, rosemary, thyme, and garlic. Bring to a boil over high heat. Reduce the heat to low and add the meat. Simmer, using tongs to turn the meat once or twice, until warmed through, about 2 minutes.

3 next **make the dip**

Meanwhile, put the bouillon cubes in a microwave-safe pitcher and add 2 cups (16 fl oz/500 ml) water. Microwave on high (100%) power until steaming hot, about 1½ minutes. Measure out ¼ cup (2 fl oz/60 ml) of the soy sauce mixture from the beef and add it to the broth; drain the beef in a colander set in the sink.

4 finally **serve the sandwiches**

Divide the broth between 4 individual bowls and place each bowl on a plate. Remove the rolls from the oven and discard the aluminum foil. Using tongs, divide the roast beef evenly among the roll bottoms, then top with the roll tops. Cut each sandwich in half and place 2 halves on each plate. Serve hot. Dip the sandwiches into the broth before taking a bite.

Makes 4 sandwiches

did you know?

Traditional club sandwiches are always served as "double-deckers" like this one. If it seems like too much of a mouthful, just "hold the club" and remove the middle slice of bread.

turkey club sandwiches

1 first cook the bacon

You can cook the bacon in a microwave or in a frying pan on the stove top. To microwave the bacon, place it in a single layer between 2 layers of paper towels on a microwave-safe plate and cook on high (100%) power until crisp, about 3 minutes. To fry the bacon, heat a 10-inch (25-cm) frying pan over medium heat. Lay the bacon in the pan and cook, using tongs to turn it over, until golden and crisp on both sides, 3–5 minutes per side. Transfer the bacon to a paper towel–lined plate to drain.

2 then make the sandwiches

Toast the bread slices in a toaster until golden. To make the first sandwich, spread ½ tablespoon mayonnaise over 1 bread slice. Using a dinner knife, cut the avocado into thin slices and place half of the slices on the bread over the mayonnaise. Arrange 2 slices of turkey in an even layer over the avocado. Spread ½ tablespoon of mayonnaise over another slice of bread, then turn it over and spread the second side with an additional ½ tablespoon mayonnaise. Place it over the turkey. Top with a lettuce leaf and half the tomato slices. Break the bacon strips in half and arrange 3 pieces of bacon in a single layer over the tomatoes. Spread a third bread slice with ½ tablespoon mayonnaise. Place it, mayonnaise side down, on top of the bacon, pressing down gently. Repeat to make the second sandwich.

3 finally serve the sandwiches

Cut the sandwiches in half on the diagonal. Serve right away.

Makes 2 sandwiches

biscuit-wrapped hot dogs

1 first prepare the dough

Preheat the oven to 450°F (230°C). Line a baking sheet with parchment paper. Place the biscuit dough on a floured work surface. Using a rolling pin, roll out the dough into a 10-by-15-inch (25-by-38-cm) rectangle about ⅓ inch (9 mm) thick, sprinkling flour on the dough as needed to prevent sticking. Cut the rectangle into six 5-inch (13–cm) squares.

2 then wrap the hot dogs

Sprinkle each dough square with 1 tablespoon of the cheese. Place a hot dog in the center of a dough square on the diagonal. Lift one uncovered corner of the square up and over the hot dog, and press it gently in place. Brush the top of the dough point on the hot dog with water, then lift the opposite corner up and over, nestling it snugly around the hot dog and wrapping it over the first dough layer, pressing gently to help it adhere. Repeat with the remaining hot dogs and dough squares. Place each wrapped hot dog, seam side up and spaced well apart, on the prepared baking sheet.

3 finally bake the hot dogs

Bake until the dough is golden brown, 10–13 minutes. Remove from the oven, let cool slightly, then serve warm.

✳ variation pig-in-a-blanket dogs

You can make these dogs quickly using store-bought crescent rolls. Preheat the oven to 350°F (180°C). Separate a package of rolls into triangles (you may have extra). Line up each hot dog on the short side of a dough triangle and roll up snugly. Bake as directed.

Makes 6 servings

what you need

Baking Powder Biscuits dough (page 117) 1 recipe

All-purpose flour for dusting

Cheddar cheese 6 tablespoons (1½ oz/45 g) shredded

Hot dogs 6, each 6 inches (15 cm)

popular condiments

Ketchup, mustard, mayonnaise, and/or pickle relish

did you know?

The hot dog-eating world record holder, Joey Chestnut, can wolf down 68 franks in just 10 minutes.

sandwich "sushi"

1 first **make the spread**

In a small bowl, stir together the goat cheese, sour cream, and dill. Season with salt and pepper. Set aside.

2 then **cut the veggies**

Cut the carrot, cucumber, and bell pepper to make matchsticks. To do this, thinly slice the vegetables, and then lay the slices down flat and thinly slice them again, to make long slivers. If this is tricky, ask an adult for help!

3 next **flatten the bread**

Lay the slices of bread on a work surface. Using a rolling pin, flatten the bread so that it will be easier to roll up.

4 finally **make the "sushi"**

Using a butter knife, divide the goat cheese mixture among the flattened bread slices, and spread it all the way to the edges. On one edge of each bread slice, lay down a few of the veggie matchsticks, letting them hang over either end. Roll up the bread around the veggies, pressing so that it seals. Cut each roll into four "sushi" pieces, arrange them on a plate, and serve.

Makes 4 servings

what you need

Soft goat cheese 4 oz (125 g)
Sour cream 2 tablespoons
Dried dill 1 teaspoon
Salt and freshly ground pepper
Carrot 1 small, peeled
Cucumber 1 small
Red bell pepper ½, seeded
Sandwich bread 4 slices

did you know?

If you love fish, substitute 4 slices of smoked salmon and 4–8 cooked asparagus spears for the other veggies here. Delish!

what you need

Vegetable oil cooking spray or olive oil for greasing

Ground turkey (preferably dark meat) 1 lb (500 g)

Salt and freshly ground pepper about ¼ teaspoon *each*

Swiss or Cheddar cheese slices 8 small

Dinner rolls 8, split

Large plum tomato 1, cut into 8 thin slices

Lettuce leaves 8 bun-size

Avocado ½, sliced

popular condiments

Ketchup, mustard, mayonnaise, and/or pickle relish

did you know?

Benjamin Franklin wanted to make the wild turkey the national bird of the United States. Political leaders chose the bald eagle instead.

mini turkey burgers

1 first prepare the grill pan

Grease a grill pan with the cooking spray or oil. Preheat the grill pan over medium-high heat.

2 then make the patties

Have ready 8 bun-size pieces of waxed paper. Place the turkey in a bowl and sprinkle with the salt and pepper. Using clean hands, mix in the seasoning, then divide the meat into 8 equal pieces. Press each piece into a patty on a piece of waxed paper, making them a little bit wider than the width of your rolls. (The patties will shrink slightly when they cook.)

3 next grill the patties and toast the rolls

Holding each patty on its piece of waxed paper, turn the patties onto the grill pan and peel off the paper. Cook until evenly browned on the bottoms, about 5 minutes. Using a metal spatula, flip over the patties. Place a slice of cheese on each patty and cook until the cheese is melted and the meat is cooked throughout, about 5 minutes longer. Using the spatula, transfer the patties to a plate. Place the rolls, cut side down, on the grill pan and cook until lightly browned, 1–4 minutes.

4 finally assemble the burgers

Place 2 roll bottoms on each of 4 serving plates. Top with the patties, melted cheese side up, and set the roll tops to the side. Place a slice of tomato, a lettuce leaf, and some of the avocado on each burger. Let everyone customize their own burgers with their favorite condiments. Serve hot.

Makes 8 small burgers; 4 servings

what you need

Salt and freshly ground pepper

Macaroni, rigatoni, or other medium tube-shaped pasta 3½ cups (12 oz/375 g)

Olive oil 1 tablespoon

Butter 3 tablespoons, plus more for greasing

Milk 1¾ cups (14 fl oz/430 ml)

All-purpose flour 3 tablespoons

White Cheddar cheese 1¼ cups (5 oz/155 g) shredded

Gruyère cheese ½ cup (2 oz/60 g) shredded

for the topping

White Cheddar cheese ¾ cup (3 oz/90 g) shredded

Panko bread crumbs ½ cup (¾ oz/20 g)

Butter 2 teaspoons, melted

crusty macaroni & cheese

1 first cook the pasta

Bring a large pot of water to a boil over high heat. Add 1 teaspoon salt and the pasta and boil until the pasta is firm but not hard, 5–7 minutes. Drain in a large colander set in the sink. Rinse under cold running water, drizzle with the oil, and toss to mix. Return to the pasta pot and set aside.

2 then make the cheese sauce

Preheat the oven to 375°F (190°C). Butter six 6–fl oz (180-ml) ramekins or an 8-inch (20-cm) square baking dish. Pour the milk into a microwave-safe measuring pitcher. Microwave on high (100%) power until hot, about 1 minute. In a saucepan over medium-low heat, melt the 3 tablespoons butter. Add the flour and cook, stirring with a wooden spoon, for 2 minutes. Gradually whisk in the hot milk. Cook, stirring, until thickened, 3–4 minutes. Add the cheeses and stir until melted and hot. Stir in ¼ teaspoon salt and a generous pinch of pepper. Pour the cheese mixture over the pasta and stir to combine. Divide the macaroni and cheese evenly among the 6 ramekins or the baking dish.

3 next make the topping

In a bowl, mix together the cheese, bread crumbs, and melted butter. Sprinkle evenly over the top of the ramekins or the baking dish.

4 finally bake the macaroni and cheese

Bake until bubbling and lightly browned on top, about 20 minutes. Remove from the oven and let cool briefly before serving. Serve hot.

Makes 6 servings

broccoli & cheese stromboli

1 first ready the dough

If using store-bought pizza dough, thaw and/or bring to room temperature before using (about 20 minutes for refrigerated dough or 5 hours for frozen).

2 then make the filling

Preheat the oven to 400°F (200°C). Line a baking sheet with parchment paper. Bring a small saucepan of water to a boil over high heat. Add 1 teaspoon salt. Add the broccoli and cook for 1 minute, then drain. In a bowl, mix together the cheeses, basil (if using), and garlic powder. Finely chop the broccoli and add to the cheese mixture. Stir until evenly mixed. Season with salt and pepper.

3 next assemble the stromboli

Place the dough on a lightly floured work surface. Using a rolling pin, roll out the dough into a 14-by-4-inch (35-by-10-cm) rectangle. Arrange the dough on the prepared baking sheet. Spoon the cheese mixture in a strip 2 inches (5 cm) wide down the center of the dough. Bring the long sides of the dough up over the filling and pinch the seam and ends closed. Roll the filled dough over on the parchment, so the seam is on the bottom. Tuck the ends underneath. Pour the olive oil into a small cup and use a pastry brush to brush it all over the dough. Sprinkle with coarse salt. Cover with a kitchen towel and let rise for 15 minutes.

4 finally bake the stromboli

Bake, uncovered, until lightly browned, about 25 minutes. Remove from the oven and let cool for 10 minutes. Cut crosswise into slices. Serve warm.

Makes 1 stromboli; 4 servings

what you need

Store-bought or homemade pizza dough (page 116) for 1 pizza

Salt and freshly ground pepper

Broccoli florets 1½ cups (3 oz/90 g)

Ricotta cheese ⅔ cup (5½ oz/170 g)

Mozzarella cheese ⅔ cup (2½ oz/75 g) shredded

Fresh basil 1 tablespoon finely chopped (optional)

Garlic powder ¼ teaspoon

All-purpose flour for dusting

Olive oil 2 teaspoons

Kosher salt or coarse sea salt for sprinkling

did you know?

Some claim the stromboli originated in Philadelphia (home of the Philly cheesesteak sandwich) as a folded pizza, but others say it's named for the Italian island of Stromboli.

what you need

Store-bought or homemade pizza dough (page 116) for 1 pizza

All-purpose flour for rolling

Cornmeal for dusting

Store-bought pizza sauce about ½ cup (4 fl oz/125 ml)

Fresh basil 1–2 teaspoons finely chopped

Fresh mozzarella cheese 6 oz (185 g), thinly sliced, or ½ cup (2 oz/60 g) shredded cheese

did you know?

It's easy to vary pizza toppings. Try any of your favorites here: salami, pepperoni, ham, or sausage; spinach, olives, or fresh sliced tomatoes; pineapple or bell peppers. The sky's the limit!

pizza margherita

1 first ready the dough

If using store-bought pizza dough, thaw and/or bring to room temperature before using (about 20 minutes for refrigerated dough or 5 hours for frozen).

2 then stretch the dough

Preheat the oven to 425°F (220°C). Place the dough on a lightly floured work surface. Using a rolling pin, roll out the dough into a 12-inch (30-cm) circle. If it begins to become elastic and difficult to roll, try gently picking up the dough by the edges, and letting the weight of the dough stretch it. You can also lift the dough, place the back of your hands underneath it, and stretch it by moving your hands outward, turning the dough in a circle.

3 next add the toppings

Line a baking sheet with parchment paper and sprinkle lightly with cornmeal. Place the dough circle on the prepared baking sheet. Using a spoon, spread the sauce over the dough, leaving ½–1 inch (12 mm–2.5 cm) of the edge uncovered. Sprinkle evenly with the basil and the cheese.

4 finally bake the pizza

Bake in the lower third of the oven until the crust is golden, 12–15 minutes. Remove the baking sheet from the oven and let the pizza cool briefly. Slide the pizza onto a cutting board. Cut into wedges and serve hot.

Makes 1 pizza; 4 servings

tortellini alfredo

1 first **make the pasta sauce**

In a saucepan over medium heat, combine the cream, cheese, butter, a pinch each of salt and pepper, and the nutmeg (if using). Heat, stirring often with a wooden spoon, until the cheese and butter are melted. Reduce the heat to low and simmer, stirring occasionally, until thickened, about 15 minutes.

2 then **boil the pasta**

While the sauce is simmering, bring a large pot of water to a boil over high heat. Add 1 teaspoon salt and then the tortellini. Reduce the heat to medium-high and boil the tortellini gently until tender, 3–4 minutes or according to the package directions. Add the peas during the last 1 minute of cooking time.

3 finally **combine the pasta and sauce**

Have ready a shallow serving bowl. Drain the tortellini and peas in a colander set in the sink and then transfer them to the serving bowl. Top the tortellini with the sauce and stir, turning the pasta gently to coat it evenly with the sauce. Sprinkle with more cheese and the parsley, if using. Serve hot.

Makes 4 servings

what you need

Heavy cream ¾ cup
(6 fl oz/180 ml)

Parmesan cheese ½ cup
(2 oz/60 g) grated plus more
for sprinkling

Butter 3 tablespoons

Salt and freshly ground pepper

Ground nutmeg pinch (optional)

Store-bought refrigerated tortellini 1 package (9 oz/280 g)

Fresh or frozen peas 1 cup
(5 oz/155 g)

Fresh flat-leaf parsley
1 teaspoon minced (optional)

did you know?

Alfredo sauce was created in the early 1900s by a restaurant owner in Rome named Alfredo (of course!). Many Italians know it as "alla panna," or "with cream."

fish tacos

1 first heat the tortillas

Preheat the oven to 400°F (200°C). Wrap the tortillas in aluminum foil and place in the oven until warmed through, about 5 minutes. Turn off the oven so that the tortillas will stay warm until ready to use.

2 then make the slaw

Using a sharp knife, cut the cabbage crosswise into thin slices, then separate into shreds. Put the cabbage in a bowl and add the sour cream, lime juice, vinegar, and salt and pepper to taste. Using your hands or 2 big spoons, toss until the cabbage is evenly coated. Set aside.

3 next cook the fish

Lightly season both sides of the fish fillets with salt and pepper. Heat the oil in a nonstick frying pan over medium-high heat. When the pan is hot, carefully slip in the fillets. Watch out, as the oil may spatter! Cook until the fillets are browned on the bottoms, about 3 minutes. Using a silicone spatula, carefully turn over the fillets and continue to cook until browned on the second sides, 2–3 minutes longer. If the fish is still slightly translucent in the center, place the pan in the oven with the tortillas for a few minutes until the flesh turns opaque.

4 finally assemble the tacos

Transfer the fish to a plate. Using 2 forks, break the fish into small chunks. Unwrap the tortillas and place 2 on each of 4 plates. Spread each tortilla with 2 tablespoons of the guacamole, then top with about ⅛ of the fish chunks, ⅛ of the cabbage slaw, and about 2 tablespoons of the tomato salsa. Fold the tortillas in half to make tacos. Serve hot.

Makes 8 tacos; 4 servings

what you need

Corn tortillas 8 small

Green cabbage ½ small head

Sour cream 2 tablespoons

Fresh lime juice 1 tablespoon

White wine vinegar 1 teaspoon

Salt and freshly ground pepper

Firm white fish fillets such as mahimahi, halibut, or sea bass 1 lb (500 g)

Olive oil 1 tablespoon

Store-bought or homemade guacamole (page 76) about 1 cup (8 oz/250 g)

Store-bought fresh tomato salsa 1 cup (8 oz/250 g)

did you know?

A taco is to the Mexican people what a sandwich is to Americans. Tortillas, thin breads made from pulverized corn kernels or wheat, have been a food staple of Mexico for thousands of years.

what you need

salsa dressing (optional)

Store-bought mild tomato salsa
1 tablespoon

Red wine vinegar 1 tablespoon

Fresh lime juice 2 teaspoons

Extra-virgin olive oil
4–6 tablespoons (2–3 fl oz/
60–90 ml)

salad

Ground beef 1 lb (500 g)

Taco seasoning mix ¼ cup
(1 oz/30 g), or about ½ package

Iceberg lettuce ½ head

Plum tomatoes 3, diced

Canned black or pinto beans
1 cup (7 oz/220 g), drained
and rinsed

Avocado 1, peeled and diced

Cheddar cheese 1½ cups
(6 oz/185 g) shredded

**Tortilla chips or Crispy Tortilla
Bowls (page 119) for serving**
(optional)

did you know?

Avocados are also
known as "alligator
pears" because of their
rough skin and pear-like
shape. They are fruits, not
vegetables, and have the
highest protein content
of any fruit.

taco salad

1 first make the salsa dressing (if using)

You can make the Salsa Dressing, or skip this step and
use your own favorite salad dressing. In a small jar or other
covered container, mix the salsa, vinegar, and lime juice.
Add 4 tablespoons of the oil, cover, and shake until mixed.
Set the dressing aside. Taste and add more oil if needed.

2 then cook the taco meat

Place a large frying pan over medium heat. Add the ground
beef and cook, using a wooden spoon to break it up into
small pieces, until evenly cooked, 8–10 minutes. (Ask an
adult to help you pour off any fat from the pan if it looks
too greasy.) Add the seasoning mix and ⅔ cup (5 fl oz/160 ml)
water to the pan. Bring to a boil over high heat. Reduce the
heat to low and simmer, stirring often, until the liquid is
absorbed, about 12 minutes.

3 next assemble the salad

While the meat is cooking, cut the lettuce into slices and
separate the pieces. Divide the lettuce among 4 individual
salad bowls, then top each with equal amounts of the
tomatoes, beans, and avocado.

4 finally serve the salads

When the meat is done, use a slotted spoon to divide it
evenly among each salad, then sprinkle the cheese on top.
Spoon some of the Salsa Dressing or your favorite dressing
over each salad. Serve at once topped with tortilla chips, if
desired. (Alternatively, arrange the salad in the tortilla bowls
instead of regular bowls.)

Makes 4 servings

more mexican dishes

monday taco

Tacos consist simply of a warmed corn tortilla or store-bought taco shell filled with hot, cooked meat (usually beef, chicken, or pork) or fish topped with salsa and guacamole. Shredded lettuce, beans, and onions can also be included.

tuesday burrito

For a basic bean and cheese burrito, wrap the tortilla in foil and warm in a 400°F (200°C) oven for 5 minutes. Spread the beans in a line down the center of the tortilla and top with the cheese. Fold both ends of the tortilla over the filling then roll up the tortilla. Wrap in the foil to keep warm.

wednesday quesadilla

Melt the butter in a nonstick frying pan. Place a tortilla in the pan, sprinkle with the shredded cheese, and top with a second tortilla. Cook, turning once, until lightly golden, about 6 minutes total. Cut into wedges to serve.

thursday taquito

Top the corn tortilla with taco-spiced ground beef or chicken. Roll up the tortilla and secure with a toothpick. Ask an adult to fry it in canola oil over medium heat until golden and crisp. Drain and serve with guacamole or salsa.

friday tostada

A tostada is an open-face taco with all the fixings. Ask an adult to help you fry a tortilla: Pour the canola oil into a frying pan and heat over medium heat until hot but not smoking. Add a tortilla and fry, until golden, about 30 seconds per side. Place the tortilla on a plate and mound the beans, meat, cheese, lettuce, tomatoes, and salsa on top.

Makes 1 serving each

what you need

taco

Small corn tortilla or taco shell 1

Hot cooked chicken or steak pieces, or cooked taco-spiced ground beef
1–2 tablespoons

Salsa and guacamole 1 tablespoon *each*

burrito

Large flour tortilla 1

Warm black or pinto beans
2 tablespoons, rinsed and drained

Monterey Jack or Colby cheese
2 tablespoons shredded

quesadilla

Butter 1 tablespoon

Large flour tortillas 2

Monterey Jack, Colby, or Cheddar cheese ½ cup (2 oz/60 g) shredded

Optional add-ins Cooked chicken or steak pieces; avocado and salsa for serving

taquito

Corn tortilla 1

Taco-spiced ground beef or chicken
2 tablespoons

Canola oil for deep-frying

Guacamole or salsa for serving

tostada

Small flour or corn tortilla 1

Canola oil 1–2 tablespoons

Warm black or pinto beans
1 tablespoon

Taco-spiced ground beef
2 tablespoons

Cheddar cheese 1 tablespoon shredded

Iceberg lettuce 1 tablespoon shredded

Chopped tomatoes or salsa
1 tablespoon

Snacks

big cheese twists

1 first **thaw the pastry**

Let the frozen puff pastry thaw at room temperature until softened, about 40 minutes.

2 then **prepare the ingredients**

Meanwhile, preheat the oven to 400°F (200°C). Line a baking sheet with parchment paper. Crack the egg into a small bowl or cup. Add 1 tablespoon water, and whisk until blended. In another small bowl, mix together the cheeses.

3 next **make the twists**

Unfold the thawed puff pastry sheet and place on a lightly floured work surface. Using a pastry brush, brush some of the egg mixture evenly over the dough. Sprinkle half of the cheese mixture evenly over half of the egg-brushed dough. Fold the uncovered dough over the cheese and press gently to seal. Brush the top with the egg mixture, sprinkle with half of the remaining cheese mixture, and press gently to help it stick. Turn the dough over, brush the other side with the egg mixture, sprinkle with the remaining cheese, and press gently. Discard any remaining egg mixture. Cut the pastry lengthwise into 4 equal strips. Holding each strip by the ends, turn the ends a few times in opposite directions to make a twist. Place the twists, evenly spaced, on the baking sheet.

4 finally **bake the twists**

Bake until browned, about 10 minutes. Let cool briefly. Serve warm or at room temperature.

Makes 4 twists

what you need

Frozen puff pastry 1 sheet

Large egg 1

Italian cheese blend, such as Parmesan, Romano, and Asiago ½ cup (2 oz/60 g) shredded

Mozzarella cheese ½ cup (2 oz/60 g) shredded

All-purpose flour for dusting

did you know?

If the twists are soft and limp once shaped, refrigerate them for about 15 minutes before baking. Keeping the pastry cold prevents the butter from melting and ensures distinct, flaky layers will form.

what you need

Pecans ¾ cup (3 oz/90 g) chopped

Soft caramel candies 1 bag (14 oz/440 g)

Apples such as McIntosh, Honeycrisp, Granny Smith, or Fuji 4, cored and quartered

did you know?

Archaeologists have found that humans have been eating apples since about 6500 bc. There are now more than 7,500 varieties of apples worldwide.

nut-dipped caramel apples

1 first toast the nuts

Preheat the oven to 350°F (180°C). Spread the nuts in a single layer on a baking sheet. Toast the nuts in the oven until golden and fragrant, about 8 minutes. Transfer the nuts to a shallow bowl or plate and set aside.

2 then melt the caramels

Unwrap the caramels and place them in a small saucepan. Add 2 tablespoons water and place over medium heat. Cook, stirring occasionally, until melted and smooth, 5–7 minutes. Keep warm over low heat.

3 next dip the apples

Line a baking sheet with waxed paper. Dip half of an apple quarter into the caramel, letting the excess caramel drip back into the pan. Roll the caramel-coated part of the apple in the nuts, pressing it gently to help the nuts adhere, and place on the baking sheet. Repeat with the remaining apples. Let stand until the caramel has set, about 10 minutes.

4 finally serve the apples

Enjoy the apples right away or wrap the quarters individually in waxed paper and store in the refrigerator for up to 1 day. Bring to room temperature before serving.

Makes 16 apple quarters; 4 servings

sweet & salty seeds

1 first mix the glaze

Preheat the oven to 350°F (180°C). Line a baking sheet with parchment paper. Put the butter into a large microwave-safe bowl. Microwave on high (100%) power until melted, 10–15 seconds. Add the honey and cinnamon and stir until blended. Add the pumpkin seeds, pine nuts, and sunflower seeds. Stir until evenly coated.

2 then bake the seeds

Spread out the seeds on the prepared baking sheet. (Use hands moistened with water to help spread out the seeds, if necessary.) Bake just until golden, 5–6 minutes.

3 finally sprinkle with salt

Remove the pan from the oven. Carefully transfer the parchment paper holding the seeds to a wire cooling rack and let cool. When cool enough to handle, break up the seed clusters with your hands and transfer to a serving bowl. Sprinkle with salt to taste and serve.

Makes 1½ cups (7 oz/220 g) glazed nuts; 4–6 servings

what you need

Butter 1 tablespoon

Honey 2 tablespoons

Ground cinnamon ¾ teaspoon

Raw pumpkin seeds (pepitas) ¾ cup (3 oz/90 g)

Pine nuts ½ cup (2½ oz/75 g)

Raw sunflower seeds ¼ cup (1 oz/30 g)

Coarse sea salt or kosher salt for sprinkling

did you know?

Pine nuts are actually the edible seeds from pinecones. All pine trees produce seeds, but many varieties produce seeds that are too small to harvest.

what you need

Sourdough baguette 1

Butter ¼ cup (2 oz/60 g)

Garlic cloves 3 large, minced (about 1½ teaspoons)

Fresh flat-leaf parsley ½ teaspoon minced (optional)

Mozzarella cheese, 1½ cups (6 oz/185 g) shredded

cheesy garlic bread

1 first **make the garlic butter**

Preheat the oven to 450°F (230°C). Ask an adult to help you cut the baguette lengthwise into two halves. In a small microwave-safe bowl or cup, combine the butter and garlic. Microwave on high (100%) power until the butter is melted, about 20 seconds. Stir in the parsley, if using.

2 then **brush the bread**

Place the bread on a baking sheet, cut sides up. Using a pastry brush, brush the butter mixture evenly over the cut sides of the baguette. Top each with an equal amount of the cheese, distributing it evenly.

3 finally **bake the bread**

Bake until the cheese is melted and the edges have turned golden brown, 5–7 minutes. Remove from the oven and let cool slightly. Cut crosswise into thick slices and serve hot.

Makes 6 servings

did you know?

Ancient cultures such as the Romans and Greeks thought that eating garlic gave them uncommon strength, so they ate it before going to battle.

what you need

Mayonnaise ½ cup
(4 fl oz/125 ml)

Low-fat buttermilk ½ cup
(4 fl oz/125 ml)

Flat-leaf parsley
1 tablespoon minced fresh, or
1 teaspoon dried parsley

Shallot 1 teaspoon minced,
or ½ teaspoon onion powder

Garlic clove 1, minced,
or ½ teaspoon garlic powder

Salt and freshly ground pepper

popular dippers

**Raw cucumber spears or slices,
carrots, snow peas, celery sticks,
jicama sticks, cauliflower florets,
broccoli florets, zucchini slices,
and bell pepper strips**

ranch-style dip
with dippers

1 first mix the dip

In a bowl, combine the mayonnaise, buttermilk, parsley,
shallot, garlic, ½ teaspoon salt, and ¼ teaspoon pepper. Stir
until blended. Taste and adjust the seasonings, if needed.

2 then serve with the dippers

Transfer the dip to a serving bowl. Serve cold or at room
temperature with your favorite dippers. Store any leftover
dip in a covered container in the refrigerator for up to 3 days.

Makes about 1 cup (8 oz/250 g)

did you know?

In 1954, the owners of Santa
Barbara's Hidden Valley
Ranch started selling their
popular salad dressing to
guests. Ranch dressing
is still a hit today.

guacamole

1 first **mash the avocado**

In a bowl, combine the avocado, lime juice, and garlic. Using the tines of a fork, mash the mixture until just smooth with some chunky avocado bits still left for texture. Add the tomato and stir to blend. Add a few dashes of the hot-pepper sauce and a sprinkling of salt and pepper. Taste and adjust the seasonings.

2 then **serve the guacamole**

Spoon the guacamole into a serving bowl and serve at room temperature with the tortilla chips or vegetables.

Makes 1 heaping bowl; 4–6 servings

what you need

Avocados 2, halved, pitted, and diced

Fresh lime juice 2 teaspoons

Garlic cloves 2, minced

Plum tomato ½, chopped

Hot-pepper sauce such as Tabasco

Salt and freshly ground pepper

Tortilla chips or vegetable sticks for dipping

did you know?

Avocados were a favorite of the Aztecs of central Mexico, who liked the fruit's creamy flavor and high fat content. For extra zing, try adding finely chopped onion, minced jalapeño chile, or chopped fresh cilantro to the mix.

cheese nachos

1 first layer the toppings on the chips

Preheat the oven to 350°F (180°C). Spread the chips in a single layer on a baking sheet. In a bowl, add the cheese and any desired toppings, except for the avocado, if using. Toss to combine. Sprinkle the cheese mixture evenly over the chips.

2 then bake the nachos

Bake the nachos until the cheese has melted and the toppings have warmed through, 12–15 minutes.

3 finally serve the nachos

Transfer the nachos to a large serving plate. Serve hot. Let everyone add salsa and sour cream as desired.

Makes 4–6 servings

what you need

Tortilla chips 6 oz (185 g)

Monterey Jack or Cheddar cheese 2 cups (8 oz/250 g) shredded

popular toppings

Black beans, kidney beans, corn, chopped tomato, chopped red or green bell pepper, black olives, finely chopped red onion, canned green chiles, and/or chopped avocado

Store-bought salsa for serving

Sour cream for serving

did you know?

Nachos were invented in Mexico in 1943 by a man named Ignacio Anaya. In Spanish, the name Ignacio is often shortened to just "Nacho"—which is how this popular snack got its name.

did you know?

Most yams sold in the United States are actually sweet potatoes. True yams are rough and scaly edible roots of a tropical vine. They are generally sweeter than regular sweet potatoes, but they are hard to find in markets.

sweet potato chips

1 first slice the sweet potatoes

Preheat the oven to 400°F (200°C). Line a baking sheet with parchment paper. Asking an adult to help you, and using a mandoline, the slicing disk on a food processor, or a knife and a very steady hand, slice the sweet potato crosswise into ⅛-inch (3-mm) slices. Put the slices in a large bowl and drizzle with the olive oil. Using your hands, toss the slices very gently to coat evenly with the oil.

2 then bake the slices

Spread the potato slices in a single layer, overlapping as little as possible, on the prepared baking sheet. Use a pastry brush, if needed, to spread the oil over any uncoated slices. Bake for 10 minutes. Remove the pan from the oven. Using a spatula, turn over all the slices. Sprinkle with ¼ teaspoon salt. Return to the oven and bake until dry and some slices are slightly browned, about 10 minutes longer. Check the slices often during the last few minutes of baking and remove them from the oven if they begin to get too brown.

3 finally serve the chips

Remove the chips from the oven and slide into a serving bowl. Sprinkle with a little more salt and serve warm.

Makes 2 servings

what you need

Salt 1 teaspoon

Thin spaghetti ½ package
(8 oz/250 g)

Soy sauce 3 tablespoons

Sesame oil 2 tablespoons

Safflower or canola oil
2 tablespoons

Sugar 1½ tablespoons

Rice vinegar 1½ tablespoons

Green onions 3 thinly sliced
or shredded

Toasted sesame seeds
2 teaspoons

sesame noodles

1 first **cook the noodles**

Bring a large pot of water to a boil. Add the salt, then add
the spaghetti, stirring gently at first so the strands don't
stick together. Boil until the spaghetti is firm but not hard,
6–8 minutes or according to the package directions.

2 then **mix the sauce**

While the pasta is cooking, in a small saucepan, combine
the soy sauce, sesame oil, safflower oil, 2 tablespoons hot
water, sugar, and vinegar. Bring to a simmer over medium
heat, stirring, until the sugar is dissolved.

3 finally **toss the ingredients**

When the pasta is ready, drain it in a colander set in the sink,
then transfer to a serving bowl. Pour the soy sauce mixture
over the top and, using a serving fork and spoon, toss until
the noodles are evenly coated with sauce. Sprinkle with the
green onions and sesame seeds. Serve warm, at room
temperature, or chilled.

Makes 4 servings

did you know?

Serve these yummy
noodles plain or add
thin strips of carrot,
crunchy snow peas,
or slices of crisp-
cooked asparagus.

fruit & nut granola bars

1 first prepare the pan

Preheat the oven to 350°F (180°C). Butter an 8-by-12-inch (20-by-30-cm) baking dish, line it with parchment paper, and butter the paper.

2 then toast the ingredients

On a rimmed baking sheet, combine the oats, almonds, pumpkin seeds, and sunflower seeds. Bake, stirring once or twice, just until golden, about 8 minutes. Transfer to a large bowl. Mix in the currants and cranberries. Set aside.

3 then mix the granola

Reduce the oven temperature to 300°F (150°C). In a small saucepan, combine the honey, sugar, butter, vanilla, and salt. Bring to a boil over medium heat, stirring often, for about 30 seconds, or until the butter is melted. Pour over the oat-fruit mixture and stir gently until evenly coated. Scoop the mixture into the prepared pan and let cool slightly. Using damp hands, press the granola into an even layer.

4 next bake the granola

Bake until golden around the edges, about 20 minutes. Let the pan cool on a wire rack for 10 minutes. Lift the paper and granola from the pan and place directly onto the rack. Let cool completely.

5 finally cut out the bars

Cutting out the bars can be tricky, so ask an adult to help you. Make 3 evenly spaced lengthwise cuts and 3 evenly spaced crosswise cuts across the granola. Serve at room temperature. Store in an airtight container for up to 5 days.

Makes 16 granola bars

what you need

Butter 3 tablespoons, plus more for greasing baking dish

Rolled oats 2 cups (6 oz/185 g)

Raw whole almonds 1 cup (5½ oz/170 g)

Raw pumpkin seeds (pepitas) ½ cup (2 oz/60 g)

Raw sunflower seeds ¼ cup (1 oz/30 g)

Dried currants or raisins ½ cup (3 oz/90 g)

Dried cranberries ½ cup (3 oz/90 g)

Honey ⅔ cup (8 oz/250 g)

Golden brown sugar ¼ cup (2 oz/60 g) firmly packed

Vanilla extract 1 teaspoon

Salt ¼ teaspoon

did you know?

Substitute any of your favorite dried fruits or nuts for the ones listed here. Try raw unsalted peanuts instead of the almonds or pumpkin seeds. Or, swap in dried cherries or chopped dried apricots for the currants or cranberries.

what you need

All-purpose flour 2 cups
(10 oz/315 g), plus more
for dusting

Baking powder 1 tablespoon

Sugar 2 teaspoons

Salt 1 teaspoon

**Dried cherries, cranberries, or
strawberries** ½ cup (2 oz/60 g)

Heavy cream ¾ cup plus
2 tablespoons (7 fl oz/215 ml)

for the topping

Heavy cream 1 tablespoon

Sugar 1 tablespoon

did you know?

Scones like these have been
a part of English teatime for
decades, although the dried
fruits give these sweet biscuits
modern appeal.

heart-shaped scones

1 first mix the ingredients

Preheat the oven to 425°F (220°C). In a large bowl, whisk
together the flour, baking powder, sugar, and salt. Add the
dried fruit and cream. Using a large spoon, stir just until
combined. Using your hands, gently gather the dough
together, kneading it against the side of the bowl until
it holds together in a rough ball.

2 then roll and cut the dough

Turn out the dough onto a lightly floured work surface. Using
a rolling pin, roll out the dough to a thickness of about ¾ inch
(2 cm). Using a 3-inch-wide (7.5-cm-wide) heart-shaped cookie
cutter, cut shapes in the dough, spacing them as closely
together as possible. Place the dough hearts at least 2 inches
(5 cm) apart on an ungreased baking sheet. Gather up the
remaining dough into a ball and knead briefly on the lightly
floured work surface. Roll out the remaining dough, cut to
make more hearts, and place on the baking sheet.

3 next add the topping

Pour the cream into a small cup. Using a pastry brush, lightly
brush the tops of the hearts with the cream, then sprinkle
evenly with the sugar.

4 finally bake the scones

Bake the hearts until golden, 10–12 minutes. Transfer to
a wire rack to cool. Serve warm or at room temperature.

Makes 10 scones

orange-cream yogurt pops

what you need

Sugar 2 tablespoons
Salt
Greek yogurt 1 cup (8 oz/250 g)
Frozen orange juice concentrate
1 cup (8 fl oz/250 ml), thawed
Wooden craft sticks 4–6

1 first **make the yogurt mixture**

In a bowl, combine the sugar, a pinch of salt, and the yogurt. Add the orange juice concentrate and stir to combine.

2 then **fill the molds**

Divide the yogurt mixture among 6 ice pop molds or 4 paper cups. Tap the bottom of the mold on the countertop to settle the mixture. Place in the freezer. After 1 hour, place a craft stick in the center of each mold.

3 finally **freeze the pops**

Return the molds to the freezer and freeze the pops until firm, at least 3 hours or up to 3 days. To remove the pops from the molds, dip the bottom of the molds into a bowl of very hot water until the pops are loosened, 10–20 seconds. (Alternatively, peel off the paper cups.) Serve at once or wrap and store in the freezer for up to 1 week.

* variation **strawberries and cream**

Instead of orange juice concentrate, use strawberry purée: Pour 2½ cups (10 oz/315 g) of hulled, halved strawberries into a blender. Add ½ cup (4 fl oz/125 ml) water and 1 teaspoon lemon juice. Purée until smooth.

* variation **peaches and cream**

Instead of orange juice concentrate, use peach purée: Pour 2½ cups (15 oz/470 g) of peeled, chopped peaches into a blender. Add ½ cup (4 fl oz/125 ml) water and 1 teaspoon lemon juice. Purée until smooth.

Makes 4–6 pops

did you know?

You can freeze pops in lots of different shapes! Try ice cube trays, nonstick muffin pans, silicone cupcake cups, or madeleine or mini brioche pans.

what you need

Agave nectar or honey ¼ cup
(3 oz/90 g)

Golden brown sugar
2 tablespoons firmly packed

**Creamy peanut butter or other
nut butter** ¼ cup (2½ oz/75 g)

Puffed rice cereal 1¾ cups
(2 oz/30 g)

Butter for greasing

did you know?

Agave nectar is a syrup made
from the agave, a cactus-like
plant from Mexico. Agave nectar
is a natural sweetener similar to
honey, but is milder in flavor and
slightly thinner in consistency.

peanutty rice puffs

1 first mix it up

In a small saucepan over medium heat, combine the agave
nectar and brown sugar. Heat, stirring, until the mixture
begins to boil and the brown sugar dissolves, 2–3 minutes.
Remove from the heat. Add the peanut butter and stir until
blended and smooth. Add the cereal and stir gently until
evenly coated. Set the mixture aside until cool enough to
handle, about 5 minutes.

2 then make the puffs

Lightly grease a rimmed baking sheet. Dampen your hands
with water to prevent sticking. Using a spoon, scoop up a
tablespoon or so of the cereal mixture and use your hands
to press it into a 1½-inch (4-cm) ball (just a bit smaller than
a golf ball). Place the ball on the baking sheet. Continue to
scoop and mold the remaining cereal mixture into balls,
placing them evenly apart on the baking sheet. (You should
have about 20 balls.)

3 next chill the puffs

Place the baking sheet in the refrigerator and chill the balls
until set, 5–10 minutes.

4 finally serve the puffs

Remove the rice balls from the refrigerator and transfer to
a serving plate or bowl. Serve at once, or store in an airtight
container at room temperature for up to 3 days.

Makes about 20 puffs

kettle corn

what you need

Vegetable oil 2 tablespoons

Sugar 2 tablespoons

Unpopped popcorn kernels
¼ cup (1½ oz/45 g)

1 first pop the corn kernels

In a large high-sided saucepan or pot over medium heat, heat the oil. Add the sugar and stir with a wooden spoon just until it begins to bubble, 1–2 minutes. Add the corn kernels and stir until well coated with the sugar. Cover tightly and cook, lifting the pan and giving it a hard shake every 10 seconds or so, until the kernels begin to pop, 2–3 minutes. (Ask an adult to help you, if necessary.) Continue to cook and shake every 5 seconds or so until the kernels have stopped popping, 1–2 minutes. If the mixture smells like it's burning, remove the pan from the heat and shake continuously until the kernels stop popping.

2 then serve the popcorn

Remove the pan from the heat and wait until all popping has stopped. Uncover the pan and, using the wooden spoon, stir the popcorn to coat it evenly with any sugar remaining on the bottom of the pan. Pour the popcorn into a bowl and serve hot.

Makes 4 servings

did you know?

The oldest evidence of popcorn was found in the Bat Cave of New Mexico, where ears of popped corn were found to be more than 4,000 years old.

lunch box snacks

monday bite-size sandwiches

Roll-ups, slices, and quarters make terrific snack sandwiches. Try rolling up turkey and cheese slices in a large flour tortilla, or broccoli and cheese in pizza dough (page 116), then slicing them into bite-size pieces. PB&J sandwich quarters and mini bagels stuffed with cream cheese are other options.

tuesday home-baked treats

Muffins are great in a lunch box. Try blueberry (page 32) or pumpkin (page 33). In the Snacks chapter, look for Big Cheese Twists (page 68), Fruit & Nut Granola Bars (page 82), and Peanutty Rice Puffs (page 87).

wednesday nibbles

Fresh nibbles like chunks of seasonal fruit and steamed edamame are healthy choices. You can also try olives, pickles, cheese, nuts, trail mix, Sweet & Salty Seeds (page 72), Sweet Potato Chips (page 79), or Kettle Corn (page 88). Hard-boiled eggs also store well through the day.

thursday dips & dippers

Pack your favorite dip or dressing for vegetables, nut butters for fruit and vegetables, and caramel sauce (page 71) for apple and pear slices. Fresh salsa, Guacamole (page 76), and Tsatsiki (page 119) are great for pita or tortilla chips.

friday from the thermos

A thermos is the best place to keep snacks hot (or cold!). For hot items, warm the thermos with hot water, then drain and wipe dry, before adding your favorite soup, pasta, or hot drink. Use a thermos to keep smoothies cold.

what you need

bite-size sandwiches

Plastic wrap or waxed paper for wrapping sandwich pieces

Long-serrated knife for cutting sandwiches

home-baked treats

Deep plastic containers or lock-top plastic bags for muffins, cookies, crackers, and rice puffs

Plastic wrap for muffins and cheese twists

Waxed paper or parchment paper for granola bars

nibbles

Bento box for keeping multiple items separate

Various plastic containers for fruit, vegetables, cheese, nuts, hard-boiled eggs, and edamame

Zippered plastic bags for Kettle Corn and Sweet Potato Chips

dips & dippers

Small plastic containers for dips

Zippered plastic bags for dippers

from the thermos

Short insulated containers for soups, chilis, and pastas

Tall insulated containers with cups for soups, hot drinks, or smoothies

Sweets

what you need

Butter ¾ cup (6 oz/185 g), at room temperature, plus more for greasing

All-purpose flour 2¼ cups (11½ oz/360 g), plus more for dusting

Baking powder 1 tablespoon

Salt ¼ teaspoon

Sugar 1¾ cups (14 oz/440 g) plus 2 tablespoons

Vanilla extract 2 teaspoons

Large eggs 3, at room temperature

Milk 1⅓ cups (11 fl oz/345 ml), at room temperature

Unsweetened cocoa powder ⅓ cup (1 oz/30 g)

Baking soda ¼ teaspoon

Chocolate Fudge Frosting (page 118) 1 recipe

did you know?

The swirly cake layers mimic the mesmerizing mixture of light and dark colors often found in glass marbles. It is also commonly known as marble cake.

chocolate swirl cake

1 first prepare the pans and begin to mix

Preheat the oven to 350°F (180°C). Butter and flour two 8-inch (20-cm) round cake pans. In a bowl, stir together the flour, baking powder, and salt. Set aside. In a large bowl, using an electric mixer, beat the butter, the 1¾ cups sugar, and the vanilla on medium speed until creamy, about 3 minutes.

2 then make the two batters

Add the eggs to the butter mixture, one at a time, beating after each addition. With the mixer on low speed, beat in one-third of the flour mixture. Add half of the milk and beat until blended. Repeat these steps, then beat in the remaining flour mixture. Scoop 2 cups (16 fl oz/500 ml) of the batter into a bowl. In a small bowl, stir together the cocoa powder and ¼ cup (2 fl oz/60 ml) hot water until smooth. Stir in the 2 tablespoons sugar and the baking soda, then add to 1 portion of the batter and mix well.

3 next swirl the batters and bake the cake

Divide the vanilla batter between the prepared pans. Scoop half of the chocolate batter on top of each. Using a thin spatula, gently draw swirls through the batters to create a marbled effect. Bake until a toothpick inserted into the center of each cake comes out clean, 30–35 minutes. Transfer the cakes to wire racks and let cool completely.

4 finally frost the cake and serve

Invert 1 cake layer onto a plate and remove the pan. Using an icing spatula or smooth knife, spread about one-third of the frosting evenly over the top. Invert the second layer onto a plate, then position on top of the first layer. Spread frosting around the sides of the cake, then frost the top. Cut into wedges and serve.

Makes 10–12 servings

pinwheel cookie lollipops

1 first mix the dough

Preheat the oven to 350°F (180°C). Lightly butter a baking sheet. In a large bowl, combine the butter, powdered sugar, and vanilla. Using an electric mixer, beat on low speed until blended, then raise the speed to medium-high and beat until creamy and pale in color, about 2 minutes. Beat in the flour on low speed until blended and smooth.

2 then tint and roll out the dough

Turn out the dough onto a lightly floured work surface and gather into a ball. Divide the ball in half. Place one half in a small bowl and add about 15 drops of yellow food coloring. Using a fork, mix the color into the dough until evenly blended. Place on a large sheet of waxed paper. Using a rolling pin, roll out into a 4-by-8-inch (10-by-20-cm) rectangle. Tint and roll out the second half of the dough the same way using a different color. Place the second sheet of dough over the yellow sheet and press firmly. Peel off waxed paper.

3 next roll up and cut the dough

Beginning at a short end of the dough stack, carefully lift the edge of the waxed paper under the dough to roll up the dough into a cylinder. Using a large knife, cut the dough crosswise in half, then cut each half into 6 slices. Place the slices on the prepared baking sheet. Gently poke a craft stick about 1 inch (2.5 cm) deep into each slice.

4 finally bake the cookies

Bake until lightly golden on the bottoms, 10–12 minutes. Let cool on the pan for a few minutes, then transfer to a wire rack and let cool completely. Serve at room temperature. Store in an airtight container for up to 3 days.

Makes 12 cookies

what you need

Butter ¾ cup (6 oz/185 g), at room temperature, plus more for greasing

Powdered sugar ¾ cup (3 oz/90 g)

Vanilla extract 1 teaspoon

All-purpose flour 1½ cups (7½ oz/235 g), plus more for dusting

Yellow, green, and/or blue food coloring

Wooden craft sticks 12

did you know?

Look for wooden craft sticks in baking supply or craft stores, or substitute inexpensive wooden chopsticks that have been cut in half.

oatmeal-raisin cookies

1 first mix the dry ingredients

Preheat the oven to 350°F (180°C). Line 2 baking sheets with parchment paper. In a bowl, stir together the flour, baking powder, cinnamon, and salt. Set aside.

2 then cream the butter and sugars

In the bowl of an electric mixer, combine the butter and sugars. Beat on low speed until combined, then raise the speed to medium and beat until light and fluffy, about 3 minutes.

3 next combine the ingredients

Using a rubber spatula, scrape down the sides of the bowl with the butter mixture. Add the eggs, one at a time, beating well after each addition. Add the vanilla and beat to combine. Reduce the speed to low and gradually add the flour mixture and the rolled oats, beating just until combined. Add the raisins and use a wooden spoon or spatula to fold them in until evenly distrubuted.

4 finally bake the cookies

Using a large spoon, scoop up round, heaping tablespoons of dough and place them 3 inches (7.5 cm) apart on the baking sheets. Bake until lightly browned, 15–20 minutes. Let the cookies cool on the pans for 5 minutes, then transfer to wire racks and let cool completely.

Makes 24 cookies

what you need

All-purpose flour 1½ cups (7½ oz/235 g)

Baking powder 1 teaspoon

Ground cinnamon 1 tablespoon

Salt ¼ teaspoon

Butter ½ cup (4 oz/125 g), at room temperature

Dark brown sugar 1 cup (7 oz/220 g) firmly packed

Granulated sugar ½ cup (4 oz/125 g)

Large eggs 2

Vanilla extract 2 teaspoons

Rolled oats 1½ cups (4½ oz/140 g)

Raisins 2 cups (12 oz/375 g)

did you know?

The famous dictionary writer Samuel Johnson once defined oats as a grain eaten by horses in England and by people in Scotland. If he were alive today, Dr. Johnson would eat his words; oats are both healthy and delicious, especially when baked in cookies and other treats.

what you need

All-purpose flour 3¾ cups (19 oz/590 g)

Baking soda 1¼ teaspoons

Salt 1 teaspoon

Butter 1¼ cups (10 oz/ 315 g), at room temperature

Golden brown sugar 1 cup (7 oz/220 g) firmly packed

Granulated sugar ¾ cup (6 oz/185 g)

Large eggs 3

Vanilla extract 2 teaspoons

Large chocolate chunks or chocolate chips 1 bag (10–11½ oz/315–360 g)

Pecans or walnuts 1 cup (4 oz/125 g) chopped

did you know?

The biggest chocolate chip cookie ever made weighed 40,000 pounds (18,144 kg) and had more than 6,000 pounds (2,722 kg) of chocolate chips!

chocolate chunk cookies

1 first mix the dry ingredients

Preheat the oven to 350°F (180°C). Line 2 baking sheets with parchment paper. In a bowl, mix together the flour, baking soda, and salt. Set aside.

2 then cream the butter and sugars

In the bowl of an electric mixer, combine the butter and sugars. Beat on low speed until combined, then beat on medium speed until light and fluffy, about 3 minutes.

3 next combine the ingredients

Using a rubber spatula, scrape down the sides of the bowl with the butter mixture. Add the eggs, one at a time, beating well after each addition. Add the vanilla and beat to combine. Reduce the speed to low and gradually add the flour mixture, beating just until combined. Stir in the chocolate and nuts with a wooden spoon or spatula until evenly combined.

4 finally bake the cookies

Using a large spoon, scoop nine rough 1½- to 2-inch (4- to 5-cm) balls of dough and place at least 2 inches (5 cm) apart on a baking sheet. Repeat to fill the second baking sheet. Bake until lightly browned, 12–15 minutes. Let the cookies cool on the pans for 5 minutes, then transfer to wire racks and let cool completely. Repeat with the remaining dough.

✳ variation white chocolate macadamia nut cookies

Substitute white chocolate chips for the chocolate chunks and unsalted macadamia nuts for the walnuts.

Makes 36 large cookies

what you need

Butter ½ cup (4 oz/125 g), at room temperature

Golden brown sugar ¾ cup (6 oz/185 g) firmly packed

Granulated sugar ¼ cup (2 oz/60 g)

Creamy peanut butter ¾ cup (7½ oz/235 g)

Large egg 1

Vanilla extract ½ teaspoon

All-purpose flour 1¼ cups (6½ oz/200 g)

Unsalted raw peanuts ⅓ cup (2 oz/60 g) finely chopped

Baking soda 1 teaspoon

Salt ¼ teaspoon

Semisweet chocolate chips 1½ cups (9 oz/280 g)

Vegetable shortening 1½ tablespoons

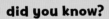

did you know?

Americans eat more than 600 million pounds of peanuts (and 700 million pounds of peanut butter) each year.

chocolate-dipped peanut butter cookies

1 first **mix the dough**

Preheat the oven to 350°F (180°C). Line 2 baking sheets with parchment paper. In a large bowl, beat the butter, brown sugar, granulated sugar, and peanut butter with an electric mixer on medium speed until blended. Add the egg and vanilla and beat until blended. Add the flour, peanuts, baking soda, and salt and beat on low speed until blended.

2 then **make the cookies**

Shape the dough into 1½-inch (4-cm) balls, placing 12 balls at least 2 inches (5 cm) apart on each baking sheet. Dip a fork in flour, then press twice into each cookie to make a crisscross pattern. Bake the cookies until golden, 8–10 minutes. Let the cookies cool on the pans for 5 minutes, then transfer to wire racks and let cool completely.

3 next **melt the chocolate**

Meanwhile, add the chocolate chips to a microwave-safe bowl. Add the shortening. Microwave on high (100%) power for 1 minute, stir gently, then microwave for 30 seconds longer or until melted.

4 finally **dip the cookies**

One at a time, dip half of each cookie into the melted chocolate, then place on a baking sheet lined with parchment paper. When all the cookies are dipped, place the baking sheet in the refrigerator just until the chocolate is set, about 5 minutes. Store the cookies in an airtight container at room temperature for up to 5 days.

Makes 24 cookies

s'more cupcakes

1 first prepare the ingredients

Preheat the oven to 350°F (180°C). Line a 12-cup muffin pan with paper liners. In a small bowl, combine the cocoa powder with ¾ cup (6 fl oz/180 ml) very hot water. Stir until blended, then add the vanilla. Set aside. In a medium bowl, stir together the flour, baking soda, and salt. Set aside.

2 then blend all the ingredients

In a large bowl, using an electric mixer, beat the butter on medium speed until shiny, about 20 seconds. Add the granulated sugar and beat until light and fluffy, about 2 minutes. Add the eggs, one at a time, beating until just blended after each addition. Beat the flour mixture into the butter-sugar mixture in 3 batches, alternating with the cocoa mixture in 2 batches.

3 next bake the cupcakes

Divide the batter evenly among the muffin cups. Sprinkle the chocolate chips evenly over the cups. Bake until a toothpick inserted into the center of a cupcake comes out clean, 17–20 minutes. Transfer to a wire rack and cool completely.

4 finally frost the cupcakes

To make the frosting, in a large bowl, using an electric mixer on medium speed, beat the butter until shiny and smooth, about 2 minutes. Add the powdered sugar and beat until smooth. Beat in the marshmallow crème just until blended. Spread the frosting on the cupcakes. Place the graham crackers in a zippered plastic bag. Using a rolling pin, roll over the crackers to make crumbs. Sprinkle the crumbs evenly over the cupcakes. Serve at room temperature.

Makes 12 cupcakes

what you need

Unsweetened cocoa powder ½ cup (1½ oz/45 g)

Vanilla extract 1½ teaspoons

All-purpose flour 1¼ cups (6½ oz/200 g)

Baking soda ½ teaspoon

Salt ½ teaspoon

Butter ¾ cup (6 oz/185 g)

Granulated sugar 1 cup (8 oz/250 g)

Large eggs 2, at room temperature

Semisweet or milk chocolate chips about ¼ cup (1½ oz/45 g)

for the frosting

Butter ½ cup (4 oz/125 g), at room temperature

Powdered sugar ½ cup (2 oz/60 g)

Marshmallow crème 1 jar (7 oz/210 g)

Graham crackers 2 whole

did you know?

The first recorded version of s'mores, the campfire favorite, was printed in the Girl Scout handbook in 1927.

what you need

Butter ¾ cup (6 oz/185 g), plus more for greasing baking pan

Unsweetened chocolate 6 oz (185 g), coarsely chopped

Large eggs 3

Sugar 1¾ cups (14 oz/440 g)

Salt ¼ teaspoon

Vanilla extract 2 teaspoons

All-purpose flour 1 cup (5 oz/155 g), plus more for dusting

did you know?

Chocolate contains serotonin, a natural body compound that transmits feelings of well-being and happiness to the brain.

ultra-chocolatey brownies

1 first **melt the butter and chocolate**

Preheat the oven to 350°F (180°C). Butter and flour an 8-inch (20-cm) square pan. Combine the butter and chocolate in a small saucepan. Place over medium heat and heat, stirring often, until melted and smooth. Set aside to cool.

2 then **mix the ingredients**

In a large bowl, whisk together the eggs, sugar, salt, and vanilla until blended. Whisk in the chocolate mixture until blended. Add the flour and whisk slowly just until blended and no lumps remain.

3 finally **bake the brownies**

Pour the batter into the prepared pan, spreading it evenly with a rubber spatula. Bake until a toothpick inserted into the center of the brownies comes out clean, 35–40 minutes. Be careful not to overbake. Transfer the pan to a wire rack and let cool. Cut into 16 squares. Serve at room temperature.

Makes 16 brownies

vanilla pound cake with fruit

1 first combine the wet ingredients

Preheat the oven to 350°F (180°C). Butter and flour a 5-by-9-inch (13-by-23-cm) loaf pan. In a large bowl, using an electric mixer on medium speed, beat the butter and sugar until creamy and pale, 3–5 minutes. Add the eggs, one at a time, beating well after each addition. Beat in the vanilla.

2 then add in the dry ingredients

In a small bowl, stir together the flour, baking powder, and salt. Beat the flour mixture into the butter mixture in 3 batches, alternating with the milk in 2 batches, beginning and ending with the flour mixture. Using a rubber spatula, scrape the batter into the prepared pan.

3 finally bake the cake

Bake until a toothpick inserted into the center comes out clean, about 1 hour. Check the cake during the last 15 minutes of baking time and drape the top with aluminum foil if it begins to get too brown. Let the cake cool on a wire rack for 10 minutes. Turn the cake out of the pan, turn back upright onto the rack, and let cool completely. Cut into slices and top with a dollop of whipped cream, if using, and a spoonful of fresh fruit. Serve at room temperature.

Makes 8–10 servings

what you need

Butter ¾ cup (6 oz/185 g), at room temperature

Sugar 1½ cups (12 oz/375 g)

Large eggs, 3

Vanilla extract 1 teaspoon

All-purpose flour 2 cups (10 oz/315 g)

Baking powder 1 teaspoon

Salt ¼ teaspoon

Milk ⅔ cup (5 fl oz/160 ml)

Whipped cream for serving (optional)

popular fruit toppings

Sliced strawberries, peaches, plums; blackberries, blueberries

did you know?

The original pound cake, which became popular in Britain in the late 1700s, was made with 1 lb (500g) each of flour, butter, sugar, and eggs.

what you need

Easy Pie Pastry (page 118) or store-bought pie dough for a single-crust pie 1

Bartlett or d'Anjou pear 1, peeled and finely chopped

Fresh lemon juice 1 teaspoon

Sugar 2 tablespoons, plus more for sprinkling

All-purpose flour 2 teaspoons, plus more for dusting

Ground cinnamon ¼ teaspoon

Ground nutmeg ⅛ teaspoon

Large egg 1, beaten with 1 tablespoon milk

did you know?

Pears have been cultivated for more than 4,000 years, and there are now over 5,000 varieties. China is the world's top producer of pears, followed by Italy and the United States.

pear hand pies

1 first **prepare the pastry and filling**

Preheat the oven to 375°F (190°C). Line a baking sheet with parchment paper. Prepare the Easy Pie Pastry (page 190) or thaw frozen pie dough just until soft enough to roll out. Place the pear in a bowl, sprinkle with the lemon juice, and toss to coat. Add the sugar, flour, cinnamon, and nutmeg. Stir gently until evenly mixed.

2 next **assemble the pies**

Divide the dough into 4 equal pieces. Work with 1 piece of dough at a time and keep the remaining dough covered with plastic wrap in the refrigerator. Place the dough piece on a lightly floured work surface. Using a rolling pin, roll out the dough into a 5-inch (13-cm) round. Spoon one-fourth of the pear mixture over half of the dough round, keeping a 1-inch (2.5-cm) border around the edge uncovered. Using a pastry brush, lightly brush the egg and milk mixture around the edges of the dough round. Fold the dough over the filling and press the tines of a fork along the seam to seal. Place the pie on the prepared baking sheet. Assemble the remaining 3 pies the same way, placing them well spaced on the baking sheet.

3 finally **bake the pies**

Brush the top of each pie with the egg and milk mixture, then sprinkle with a little sugar. Bake until golden brown, 12–20 minutes. Let cool on a wire rack. Serve warm or at room temperature.

✳ variation **apple hand pies**

Substitute a medium apple for the pear.

Makes 4 pies

peach-blackberry crisp

1 first mix the topping

Preheat the oven to 375°F (190°C). In a small bowl, stir together the oats, brown sugar, flour, nuts, cinnamon, nutmeg, and salt. Using your fingertips, rub the butter into the oat mixture until well blended and crumbly.

2 then layer the ingredients

In eight 8-oz (250-g) gratin dishes or one 9-by-12-inch (23-by-30-cm) baking dish, combine the peaches and blackberries and spread in an even layer. Scatter the topping evenly over the fruit.

3 finally bake the crisp

Bake until the juices are bubbling and the topping is richly browned, 30–35 minutes. Remove from the oven and let cool slightly. Scoop individual portions of the crisp onto serving plates or serve in the individual gratin dishes. Serve warm or at room temperature, accompanied with vanilla ice cream, if desired.

Makes 8–10 servings

what you need

Rolled oats ½ cup (1½ oz/45 g)

Golden brown sugar ½ cup (3½ oz/105 g) firmly packed

All-purpose flour ¼ cup (1½ oz/45 g)

Almonds or pecans ¼ cup (1½ oz/45 g) finely chopped

Ground cinnamon ½ teaspoon

Ground nutmeg ¼ teaspoon

Salt ¼ teaspoon

Butter 6 tablespoons (3 oz/90 g), at room temperature

Peaches 4 (about 2 lb/1 kg), peeled and sliced

Blackberries 1 cup (about 4 oz/125 g)

Vanilla ice cream for serving (optional)

did you know?

Peaches were first cultivated in China, where the peach tree is considered to be the tree of life and the fruits are symbols of longevity and unity. Chinese brides often carry peach blossoms in their wedding bouquets.

chocolate-dipped strawberries

what you need

Semisweet chocolate chips
1 cup (6 oz/185 g)

Vegetable shortening
1 tablespoon

Large strawberries 2 pints
(16 oz/500 g), rinsed

1 first **melt the chocolate**

Fill a small saucepan with about 1 inch (2.5 cm) of water and place over low heat. In a small heatproof bowl, combine the chocolate chips and shortening. Place the bowl over the pan so that it rests on the pan rim but does not touch the water below. Heat the chocolate, stirring occasionally with a rubber spatula, until melted and smooth, 5–7 minutes. Remove the pan from the heat, but leave the bowl atop the pan to keep the chocolate warm.

2 then **dip the strawberries**

Line a baking sheet with waxed paper. Holding each strawberry by its green hull or stem, dip it into the melted chocolate until it is about three-fourths covered. Use the spatula, if necessary, to help coat each strawberry with chocolate. Let the excess chocolate drip back into the bowl, then place each strawberry on the prepared baking sheet.

3 finally **chill the chocolate**

When all of the berries have been dipped, place the baking sheet in the refrigerator until the chocolate sets, 10–15 minutes. Transfer the chocolate-dipped berries to a serving plate. They are best eaten within a day. If necessary, cover loosely with waxed paper and store overnight in the refrigerator. Serve at room temperature.

Makes 2 pints dipped strawberries; 4–6 servings

did you know?

The cacao beans used to make chocolate were so valuable in ancient Mexico that the Mayans and Aztecs used them as a form of currency to pay for goods and taxes.

what you need

Large bananas 2

Butter 1 tablespoon

Greek-style yogurt 1 cup
(8 oz/250 g)

Honey for drizzling

sautéed bananas with yogurt and honey

1 first **cook the bananas**

Peel and slice the bananas. Heat a frying pan over medium heat until hot, but not smoking. Add the butter. Using a spatula, spread the butter evenly over the pan bottom. Add the sliced bananas and cook, stirring occasionally, until browned on both sides, 4–6 minutes.

2 then **assemble the dessert**

Divide the yogurt among individual bowls. Divide the bananas among the bowls, spooning the slices over the yogurt. Drizzle with honey. Serve warm.

Makes 2–4 servings

did you know?

Greek yogurt is yogurt that has been strained, making it a little more like cream cheese in texture. Rich and thick, it is perfect for sweet snacks and desserts.

frozen fruit pops

1 first **make a sugar syrup**

In a small saucepan, combine the sugar and ⅓ cup (3 fl oz/ 80 ml) water. Cook over high heat, stirring constantly, until the sugar dissolves to form a syrup, 2–3 minutes.

2 then **prepare the first layer**

Rinse the strawberries with room-temperature water. Set aside to thaw. Pour the mango cubes into a blender. Add ¼ cup (2 fl oz/60 ml) of the orange juice and 2 tablespoons of the syrup. Purée until smooth. Divide the mango purée among 6 ice pop molds or 4 paper cups. Tap the bottom of the molds on the countertop to settle the purée. Place in the freezer. After 1 hour, place a craft stick in the center of each mold.

3 then **create the second layer**

Rinse the blender. Pour the pineapple cubes into the clean blender. Add ¼ cup juice and 2 tablespoons of the syrup, purée until smooth, and pour over the mango purée in the ice pop molds or cups. Return to the freezer.

4 next **create the third layer**

Rinse the blender. Pour the strawberries into the clean blender. Add the remaining ¼ cup juice and the remaining syrup, purée until smooth, and pour over the pineapple purée in the ice pop molds or cups. Return to the freezer.

5 finally **freeze until firm**

Freeze the layered fruit pops until firm, 2–4 hours. To remove the pops from the molds, dip the bottoms in a bowl of very hot water until the pops start to loosen, about 20 seconds. (Alternatively, peel off the paper cups.) Serve at once, or wrap and store in the freezer for up to 1 week.

Makes 4–6 pops

what you need

Sugar ⅓ cup (3 oz/90 g)

Frozen strawberries 1 cup (4 oz/125 g)

Frozen mango cubes 1 cup (6 oz/185 g)

Orange juice, pineapple juice, or orange-pineapple juice blend ¾ cup (6 fl oz/180 ml)

Wooden craft sticks 4–6

Frozen pineapple cubes 1 cup (6 oz/185 g)

did you know?

Indigenous to India and cultivated in many tropical regions of the world, mangoes are bursting with nutrients. They are high in fiber, and in vitamin C (especially when young), and vitamin A (especially when ripe).

all about ice cream

monday ice cream sandwich

To soften the ice cream, let it stand on the counter for about 10 minutes. Place 1 cookie, flat side up, on a work surface and top with the scoop of ice cream. Top with the second cookie, flat side down, and push down until the ice cream reaches the cookie edges. Roll the edges in your favorite dippers. Freeze until firm.

tuesday milk shake

Place the ice cream scoops in a blender. Add enough milk to come halfway up the sides of the ice cream. Blend until smooth. Add more milk or ice cream if necessary to achieve a good consistency. Pour into a tall glass. Serve with a straw.

wednesday banana split

Cut the banana in half lengthwise and set, cut sides up, in a bowl. Top with the vanilla, chocolate, and strawberry ice cream scoops, then top with your favorite sauces, whipped cream, chopped nuts, and the cherry.

thursday ice cream float

Fill a tall glass about two-thirds full with soda pop. Carefully slip the vanilla ice cream scoops into the glass. Top with the whipped cream and serve with a long spoon and straw.

friday sundae bar

Invite your friends over and set up a sundae bar on your kitchen countertop. Start with your favorite ice creams. Don't forget whipped cream, and chocolate and caramel sauce, and your favorite toppings that you and your friends can mix and match. Create your own sundae masterpieces!

Makes 1 serving each

what you need

ice cream sandwich
Ice cream 1 large scoop

Large cookies 2

Optional dippers Chocolate or rainbow jimmies, chopped nuts, crushed cookie crumbs, or melted chocolate (page 110)

milk shake
Ice cream 3 scoops

Milk ½–1 cup (4–8 fl oz/125–250 ml)

banana split
Banana 1

Vanilla, chocolate, and strawberry ice cream 1 scoop *each*

Butterscotch sauce (page 119), chocolate sauce (page 119), and berry sauce 1 tablespoon *each*

Whipped cream about ½ cup (2 oz/60 g)

Walnuts or pecans 1 tablespoon toasted and chopped

Maraschino cherry 1

ice cream float
Soda pop 1 can (12 fl oz/375 ml)

Vanilla ice cream 1–2 scoops

Whipped cream 2 tablespoons

sundae bar
Ice cream 2 cartons or more

Whipped cream 2 canisters or more

Chocolate sauce (page 119), Butterscotch sauce (page 119)

Popular toppings Small or chopped candies, chocolate chips, cookie crumbs, chopped nuts, jimmies, fresh berries

basic recipes

pizza dough
Makes enough dough for
two 12-inch (30-cm) pizzas

Lukewarm (110°F/43°C) water 1½ cups (12 fl oz/375 ml)

Active dry yeast 1 package (2½ teaspoons)

Salt ½ teaspoon

Olive oil 1 tablespoon, plus more for greasing

All-purpose flour about 4 cups (20 oz/625 g)

make a wet dough
In a large bowl or in the bowl of a stand mixer, combine the water and yeast and let stand until foamy, about 2 minutes. Add the salt, 1 tablespoon oil, and 2½ cups (12½ oz/390 g) of the flour. Beat with an electric mixer on medium speed (using a paddle attachment on the stand mixer) until the dough is glossy and stretchy, about 5 minutes.

to knead with a mixer
On low speed, beat in about 1 cup (5 oz/155 g) more flour until combined. Remove the paddle attachment and attach a dough hook to the stand mixer. Add ¼ cup (1½ oz/45 g) more flour. Beat on low speed until incorporated, then beat on medium speed until the dough is no longer sticky and springs to the touch, 5–7 minutes. Add more flour, about 1 tablespoon at a time, only as needed to prevent sticking.

to knead by hand
Using a wooden spoon, stir in 1 cup (5 oz /155 g) more flour. Dump ½ cup (2½ oz/75 g) flour out onto a clean work surface and spread it around with your fingers until the surface is well coated. Turn the dough out onto the surface and flour your hands. With the heel of your hand, knead the dough by pulling the far half of the dough toward you, folding it over itself, then pushing the dough down and away from you along the floured work surface. Turn the dough a quarter turn and repeat the steps, pulling the dough, folding it in half, and pushing the dough with the heel of your hand. Continue to turn and knead, adding flour only as needed to prevent sticking, until the dough is no longer sticky and springs to the touch, 10–15 minutes.

let it rise
Place the dough kneaded by either method in a lightly oiled bowl and turn to coat its surface with oil. Cover with plastic wrap and let rise in a warm place until doubled in bulk, 1–1½ hours. (You can also let it rise in the refrigerator overnight. Bring to room temperature for about 1 hour before continuing.)

use in recipes
Cut the dough in half, using one half per 12-inch (30-cm) pizza.

sweet white bread
Makes one 4-by-8-inch (10-by-20-cm) loaf

Lukewarm (110°F/43°C) water ½ cup (4 fl oz/125 ml)

Active dry yeast 1 package (2½ teaspoons)

Lukewarm (110°F/43°C) milk ½ cup (4 fl oz/125 ml)

Sugar ¼ cup (2 oz/60 g)

Salt 1 teaspoon

Large egg 1

Butter ¼ cup (2 oz/60 g) plus 1 tablespoon, melted separately, plus more for greasing

All-purpose flour 3–3½ cups (15–18 oz/470–560 g)

Oil for greasing

make a wet dough
In a large bowl or in the bowl of a stand mixer, combine the water and yeast and let stand until foamy, about 2 minutes. Add the milk, sugar, and salt. Add the egg and whisk until blended. Stir in the ¼ cup melted butter and 2½ cups (12½ oz/390 g) of the flour.

to knead with the mixer

Attach a dough hook to a stand mixer. Gradually beat in ½ cup (2½ oz/75 g) more flour on low speed, then increase the speed to medium and beat until the dough is no longer sticky and springs to the touch, 3–4 minutes. Add more flour, about 1 tablespoon at a time, only as needed to prevent sticking.

to knead by hand

Dump ½ cup (2½ oz/75 g) flour out onto a clean work surface and spread it around with your fingers until the surface is well coated. Turn the dough out onto the surface and flour your hands. With the heel of your hand, knead the dough by pulling the far half of the dough toward you, folding it over itself, then pushing the dough down and away from you along the work surface. Turn the dough a quarter turn and repeat the steps, pulling the dough, folding it in half, and pushing the dough with the heel of your hand. Continue to turn and knead, adding flour only as needed to prevent sticking, until the dough is no longer sticky and springs to the touch, 5–7 minutes.

let it rise

Place the dough kneaded by either method in a lightly oiled bowl and turn to cover its surface with oil. Cover with plastic wrap and let rise in a warm place until doubled in bulk, 1–1½ hours.

shape it

Butter a 4-by-8-inch (10-by-20-cm) loaf pan. Turn out the risen dough onto a clean work surface and press down on the dough to release any air bubbles. Roll up the dough into a loaf shape and pinch the seam closed to seal. Place the loaf, seam side down and ends tucked in, into the prepared loaf pan. Brush with the remaining 1 tablespoon melted butter.

let it rise again

Cover the pan with a kitchen towel and let the dough rise again in a warm place until doubled, about 1 hour.

bake the loaf

Preheat the oven to 375°F (190°C). Bake until lightly browned and the loaf sounds hollow when gently tapped with a finger, 20–22 minutes. Let the bread cool in the pan on a wire rack for 5 minutes. Turn the loaf out onto the rack, turn upright, and let cool completely. Cut into slices before serving.

variation **cinnamon-swirl bread**

Make the Sweet White Bread dough as directed and let it rise. When shaping the dough, turn out the dough onto a clean work surface and press out the air bubbles. Using a rolling pin, roll out the dough into an 8-by-12-inch (20-by-30-cm) rectangle. In a small bowl, mix together ¼ cup (2 oz/60 g) sugar with 2 teaspoons ground cinnamon. Brush the dough rectangle with 1 tablespoon melted butter, then sprinkle evenly with the cinnamon-sugar mixture. Starting at a short end, roll up the dough into a loaf shape and pinch the seam closed to seal. Continue as directed in recipe, placing the dough in the pan, brushing the top with 1 tablespoon melted butter, then baking it at 350°F (180°C) for 32–35 minutes.

baking powder biscuits
Makes 8 biscuits

All-purpose flour 2 cups (10 oz/315 g), plus more for dusting

Baking powder 1 tablespoon

Sugar 1 teaspoon

Salt 1 teaspoon

Cold butter 7 tablespoons (3½ oz /105 g), cut into chunks

Whole milk ¾ cup (6 fl oz/180 ml)

make the biscuit dough

If using a food processor, mix the flour, baking powder, sugar, and salt in the bowl. Scatter the butter pieces over the flour mixture and pulse just until the flour begins to form small pebbles. Slowly add the milk, pulsing constantly, but just until combined into large globs of dough.

If using a mixing bowl, stir together the flour, baking powder, sugar, and salt in the bowl. Scatter the butter pieces over the flour mixture. Rub the butter into the flour by rubbing your thumb against your fingertips like you are snapping in slow motion. Continue rubbing in the butter until the mixture forms the shape of small pebbles.

finish the dough

Dump the dough out onto a well-floured work surface. Using your hands, press the dough into a single mound, kneading gently to incorporate all the flour. Use the dough as directed for individual recipes, or cut into biscuits and bake (below).

cut and bake the biscuits

Preheat the oven to 450°F (230°C). Line a baking sheet with parchment paper. Using a rolling pin, roll out the dough to about ¾ inch (2 cm) thick. Using a 3-inch (7.5-cm) round biscuit cutter, cut the dough into biscuits and place well apart on the prepared baking sheet. Gather up the scraps and knead briefly into a ball. Roll and cut again, placing the biscuits on the baking sheet. Bake until golden brown, about 10 minutes. Serve warm or at room temperature.

easy pie pastry

Makes enough pastry for 1 single-crust pie or 4 hand pies

All-purpose flour 1½ cups (7½ oz/235 g)

Sugar 1 teaspoon

Salt ½ teaspoon

Cold butter ½ cup (4 oz/125 g), cut into chunks

Ice water ¼ cup (2 fl oz/60 ml)

make the dough

In the bowl of a food processor, mix the flour, sugar, and salt. Scatter the chunks of butter over the flour mixture and pulse until coarse crumbs form. Slowly add the water, pulsing constantly, but just until well mixed and the dough begins to hold together.

form the dough

Dump the dough out onto a sheet of plastic wrap. Gather the dough up in the wrap, molding it into a ball. Flatten the ball into a 6-inch (15-cm) disk and cover evenly with the plastic wrap. Refrigerate for at least 1 hour or up to 3 days. Use as directed.

chocolate fudge frosting

Makes about 2⅔ cups (21 fl oz/655 ml), enough for 1 double-layer cake

Butter ¼ cup (2 oz/60 g)

Heavy cream ¼ cup (2 fl oz/60 ml)

Semisweet or bittersweet chocolate 2 cups (12 oz/375 g), chips or coarsely chopped

Sour cream ¾ cup (6 oz/185 g)

Powdered sugar 1¼ cups (5 oz/155 g)

melt the chocolate

In a heavy saucepan over low heat, combine the butter and cream. Heat, stirring often, until the butter melts. Add the chocolate and whisk gently until melted and smooth, about 2 minutes. Remove from the heat. Let cool to lukewarm, about 8 minutes.

whisk the mixture

Whisk in the sour cream until fully combined. Scoop the powdered sugar into a sifter and gradually sift over the chocolate mixture, whisking constantly, until no lumps remain.

cool the frosting

Place the bowl in the refrigerator and let the frosting cool and thicken, whisking every 10 minutes, until thick enough to spread, about 30 minutes. (To thicken the frosting faster, place the bowl of frosting in a larger bowl of ice and whisk until thickened.) If the frosting becomes too stiff to spread, rewarm briefly over low heat and whisk again until smooth.

chocolate sauce
Makes about 1 cup (8 fl oz/250 ml)

Heavy cream ⅔ cup (5 fl oz/160 ml)

Light corn syrup ½ cup (5 fl oz/160 ml)

Golden brown sugar 2 tablespoons firmly packed

Semisweet chocolate 5 oz (155 g), coarsely chopped

Salt pinch

Vanilla extract 1 teaspoon

make the sauce
In a heavy saucepan over medium-low heat, combine the cream, corn syrup, and brown sugar. Bring to a boil and cook, stirring occasionally until the sugar dissolves, about 5 minutes. In a bowl, combine the chocolate and salt. Pour the hot cream mixture over the chocolate and stir until melted and smooth. Add the vanilla and stir to combine. Use immediately, or let cool, cover, and refrigerate for up to 1 week. Reheat or use at room temperature or chilled.

butterscotch sauce
Makes about 1⅓ cups (11 fl oz/345 ml)

Butter 4 tablespoons (2 oz/60 g)

Golden brown sugar 1 cup (7 oz/220 g) firmly packed

Heavy cream ¾ cup (6 fl oz/180 ml)

Vanilla extract 1 tablespoon, or to taste

Kosher salt ½ teaspoon, or to taste

cook the sugar
In a small saucepan over medium-low heat, melt the butter. Add the brown sugar and, using a wooden spoon, stir until blended. Cook, stirring occasionally, until the mixture bubbles and looks like thick syrup, 3–5 minutes. Be careful as the mixture will be very hot!

whisk in the cream and add the seasonings
Add the cream and whisk until blended. Simmer over low heat, whisking occasionally, for 5 minutes. Remove from the heat and let cool to lukewarm or room temperature. Stir in the vanilla and salt. Taste and add more vanilla or salt, if you like.

serve and store
Store in a glass or ceramic container in the refrigerator for up to 1 month. Bring to room temperature or warm slightly in the microwave before serving.

tsatsiki
Makes about 2 cups (16 oz/500 g)

Plain yogurt 1 container (7 oz/220 g), preferably Greek style

Grated or finely diced English cucumber 1 cup (5 oz/155 g)

Garlic clove 1, minced

Fresh mint and fresh dill 1 teaspoon minced *each*

make the dip
In a small bowl, mix together the yogurt, cucumber, garlic, mint, and dill. Serve at once or cover and refrigerate for up to 3 days.

crispy tortilla bowls
Makes 4 tortilla bowls

8-inch (20-cm) flour tortillas 4

Vegetable oil

Salt

preheat the oven and ready the tortillas
Preheat the oven to 350°F (180°C). Choose 4 shallow ovenproof bowls about 4–6 inches (10–15 cm) in diameter. Using a pastry brush, brush vegetable oil over both sides of each tortilla and sprinkle with salt. Stuff the tortillas into the bowls to make bowl shapes.

bake the bowls
Bake the tortillas in the bowls until browned and crisp, about 12 minutes. Remove from the oven and let cool. Remove the tortillas from the bowls. Place each tortilla bowl in a shallow bowl or plate before filling with your favorite ingredients.

tools

whisk
A tool used to whip together liquid ingredients and batters smoothly.

spatula
A wide, flat tool perfect for slipping under food to flip or turn during cooking.

rolling pin
A wooden or plastic tool used to roll out dough. Some have two handles.

rubber spatula
A flexible rubber tool used to scrape down bowls and fold ingredients together.

box grater/shredder
A metal kitchen tool that makes it easy to shred cheese or grate citrus zest.

dry measuring cups
A set of cups with straight sides that make it easy to level off dry ingredients.

colander
A metal or plastic bowl with holes in it that allow liquids to drain through it.

measuring spoons
A set of spoons used to measure small amounts of dry or liquid ingredients.

ladle
A long-handled spoon with a deep bowl that is used to serve soups or stews.

liquid measuring cup
A clear glass cup that shows exactly when liquid fills up to the right mark.

saucepan with lid

Deep pans are used for stove-top cooking such as boiling or simmering.

immersion blender

A handheld blender, which can purée soup, for instance, while in the pot.

frying pan

Shallow pans are used on the stove-top for frying or cooking all kinds of food.

Cuisinart

A food processor. Different blades can slice, chop, purée, or knead doughs.

crepe pan

A very shallow specialty pan used to make thin, round French pancakes.

stand mixer

A countertop mixer with different speeds, which can beat doughs or whip eggs.

grill pan

Similar to a frying pan, but with raised ridges that sear "grill" marks onto food.

panini press

A countertop appliance that presses down to make toasty, grilled sandwiches.

mini chopper

A little food processor that quickly chops small foods like herbs, onions, or garlic.

waffle iron

An electric countertop appliance used to make round or square waffles.

tips & techniques

getting started

prepare work area & ingredients

Before you begin cooking, make sure your hands are washed and that your work area is clean. Read through the recipe from start to finish and get out any necessary kitchen equipment. Look over the ingredients list and identify if any need to be prepared before they can be measured.

wash ingredients

If you will be using any fresh fruits or vegetables that do not have peels, wash them. Most can be put into a colander and rinsed with cold running water. Greens like lettuce and spinach may need to be rinsed twice to wash away all the dirt. Others, such as potatoes, may require some scrubbing with a firm-bristled brush to loosen surface dirt before they can be rinsed clean.

grease and flour pans

Some of the recipes in this book call for greasing a pan or dish. This helps keep the food from sticking and makes cleanup easier. To do this, use a piece of paper towel to pick up a small amount of room-temperature butter or oil, then rub it all over the pan bottom. If pans must also be floured (as in some of the baking recipes), add a spoonful of flour to a greased pan, then tilt the pan back and forth until the bottom and sides are dusted with a thin layer of flour. Tap any excess flour.

knife skills

take precaution

Learning how to use a knife without hurting yourself can be one of the most important steps to becoming comfortable in a kitchen. It takes time and practice, so you might want to ask an adult to help you until you feel comfortable. Using a mini chopper or food processor can also make chopping, mincing, and slicing foods much easier.

choose the right size knife

First, make sure that the knife feels comfortable in your hand. Many adult knives are too big for little hands. A smaller knife can often accomplish the same task as a larger one.

learn to cut

Hold the knife firmly by the handle like you're shaking someone's hand. You can extend your index finger along the top of the knife to help guide it when you cut, if necessary. Hold down the item you are cutting with your other hand, placing the flat side of the food down whenever you can. (You can usually cut a little slice off a rounded edge to create a flat side.) Curl under the fingers of the hand that's holding the food so that your knuckles keep your fingers out of harm's way. With the tip of the knife pointing down, start to cut, bringing the handle down and always keeping the knife facing away from your body.

terminology

Items can be chopped into varying sizes. "Coarsely chopped" refers to items that are cut into misshapen bite-size chunks. "Finely chopped" refers to items that are cut into small pieces. "Minced" refers to items that are cut even smaller, into pieces the size of crumbs.

measuring

dry ingredients

To measure dry ingredients like flour or sugar, scoop them into a measuring cup or spoon, then level the top with your hand or the flat edge of a knife. If an ingredient needs to be firmly packed, like brown sugar, press down on the ingredient to pack it into the cup or spoon, adding more if necessary, before you've finished measuring.

wet ingredients

To measure wet ingredients, pour them into a liquid measuring cup placed on a flat surface. Check the measurement at eye level to make sure it is correct.

butter

To measure butter, simply use the measuring lines marked on the butter wrapper as your guide. Using a knife, cut off the amount of butter you need.

baking

When preparing most doughs or batters for baking, specific mixing techniques may be required.

creaming butter & sugar

Remove butter from the refrigerator and allow it to come to room temperature. When the butter is softened, combine it with the sugar in a bowl. Using an electric mixer, beat the butter and sugar until creamy and light in color. You may need to stop the mixer a couple of times and scrape down the sides of the bowl with a rubber spatula to mix the ingredients evenly.

cutting in butter

To make pastry dough, butter is "cut" or "rubbed" into a flour mixture. The butter must be well chilled, so remove it from the refrigerator just before using. Immediately cut the butter into small pieces and add it to the flour mixture. Rub the butter into the flour by rubbing your thumb against your fingertips. Continue in this manner until the butter and flour form small, pebble like pieces.

using a rolling pin

Before rolling out any dough, sprinkle a clean work surface with some flour. Place a ball of dough on the floured surface, and sprinkle the top of the dough or the rolling pin with more flour to prevent sticking. Roll out the dough from the middle to the edges, rotating the dough often and sprinkling underneath and on top with flour as needed to prevent sticking.

keeping pastry cold

Some buttery pastry doughs must be kept cold to ensure that the tiny chunks of butter hidden in the dough are solid enough to create light and flaky layers while it bakes. Make sure puff pastry and pie pastry are kept cold until just before baking, placing them in the refrigerator to chill if the dough starts to become limp and soft during rolling or shaping.

even baking

Browning baked goods evenly can be tricky, especially when there is more than one pan in the oven, or when the sugar in a particular dough makes it brown before the filling is done.

If you need to use more than one baking sheet in the oven at the same time, try switching the pan positions halfway through baking to make sure the baked items brown evenly.

To prevent overbrowning on the bottoms of baked items, line the baking pan or sheet with a layer of parchment paper, cut to the size of a pan, before adding items for baking.

To prevent overbrowning on the top of an item that is being baked, check it 5–10 minutes before the end of the baking time. Cover the top loosely with a single sheet of aluminum foil if it looks like the top will brown before baking is complete.

testing for doneness

For most baked items, a simple "toothpick test" will do the trick. Pierce the center of the item with a clean toothpick. The toothpick should come out clean. If it still has a few wet crumbs attached, return the pan to the oven and bake for just a few minutes longer or until a new toothpick inserted into the center comes out clean.

glossary

This alphabetical list includes tips and trivia, as well as the meanings of ingredients and techniques you'll find in this cookbook.

baking powder

A powdery white product made by combining baking soda, an acid such as cream of tartar, and cornstarch or flour. Used to make some doughs and batters rise during baking.

baking soda

A white chemical powder that, when combined with an acid ingredient such as sour cream or buttermilk, releases carbon dioxide, causing a batter to rise as it bakes in the oven.

bean sprouts

The sprouts of mung beans , these add fresh flavor and crisp texture to Asian dishes.

boil

To heat a liquid until bubbles constantly rise to its surface and break. A gentle boil is when small bubbles rise and break slowly. A rolling boil is when large bubbles rise and break quickly.

bouillon cubes

Cubes that can be dissolved in hot water to make a broth, which is a liquid rich with the flavors of chicken, meat, seafood, or vegetables.

buttermilk

A type of milk that is often used in desserts, baked goods, and dressings. It has a tangy flavor and thick texture similar to yogurt.

chocolate

Chocolate is available in many different forms. Semisweet chocolate is a dark, sweet chocolate sold in blocks, bars, and chips. If milk is added, it becomes milk chocolate. Unsweetened chocolate is bitter with a strong chocolate flavor; it is sold in small squares or blocks.

cocoa powder, unsweetened

A fine, bitter powder with a strong chocolate flavor; it is different from hot cocoa mix because it includes no sugar or milk products.

cornstarch

A very fine powder made by grinding the center (known as the endosperm) of corn kernels. Used as a thickener.

cream, heavy

Also called heavy whipping cream, heavy cream has a thick, rich consistency because it contains a high percentage of milk fat.

drizzle

To pour a liquid, such as oil or icing, back and forth lightly in a thin stream.

dust

To cover a food, your hands, or a work surface lightly with a powdery substance such as flour or sugar.

eggs

Sold in a range of sizes. Use eggs marked "large" for this book's recipes.

flour, all-purpose

The most common flour available, composed of a blend of wheats so that it works equally well for cakes, cookies, and other baked goods.

graham cracker

A whole-wheat, honey-sweetened rectangular cookie.

grate

To slide an ingredient, such as cheese, across a surface of small, sharp-edged holes on a grater-shredder to create tiny pieces.

grease

To rub a baking pan or dish evenly with butter or oil to prevent sticking.

heatproof

Dishes, utensils, or surfaces that can come in contact with high heat without becoming damaged.

knead

To work dough with your hands, using pressing, folding, and turning motions. When dough is fully kneaded, it becomes smooth and elastic.

marshmallow crème

A very sweet, spreadable, marshmallow-like confection often made from corn syrup, simple syrup, vanilla flavoring, and egg whites. Also known as marshmallow fluff.

oats, rolled

Whole oat grains that have been flattened and steamed.

oil, canola

A mild-tasting vegetable oil made by pressing canola seeds.

oil, olive

Flavorful cooking oil pressed from olives.

oil, safflower

A mild-tasting vegetable oil pressed from the seeds of the safflower plant, a member of the sunflower family.

panko bread crumbs

A chunky but light type of Japanese bread crumbs, which lend an exceptionally light and crisp texture to fried foods and toppings. You can find panko in Asian markets and well-stocked supermarkets.

parchment paper

A nonstick, burn-resistant paper used for baking.

parker house rolls

A bread roll made by flattening the center of a small piece of dough with a rolling pin, then folding it in half.

They are generally quite buttery, soft, and slightly sweet with a crispy shell. Frozen Parker House–style rolls are sold by the dozen in supermarkets.

pinch

The amount of a dry ingredient that you can pick up, or "pinch," between your thumb and index finger; less than ⅛ teaspoon.

salt (regular, sea, kosher)

Salt brings out the flavors of food, even sweet baked goods. Regular table salt is fine grained. Sea salt and kosher salt are categorized as coarse salts because they have larger flakes. Sea salt is gathered naturally in pans from the sea, and has a pronounced, clean flavor. Kosher salt has been pressed, which gives it large, mild flakes.

simmer

To heat a liquid to just below boiling. The surface of the liquid should be steaming and barely bubbling.

sugar (regular, powdered, brown)

The three most common sugars are granulated sugar, small, white granules that pour easily; powdered sugar, which is granulated sugar finely ground and mixed with cornstarch; and brown sugar, a moist blend of granulated sugar and molasses. Brown sugar is sold in two types: golden and dark. When a recipe calls for "sugar," use granulated sugar.

taco seasoning

A blend of Mexican seasonings that is sold in the supermarket.

tomato paste

A thick paste of puréed tomatoes that is sold in cans. Tomato paste has intense flavor, and is often used to flavor soups and sauces.

vegetable shortening

A solid white fat made from vegetable oil, which can substitute for butter. Shortening makes particularly flaky pie crusts and cookies.

whisk

To stir a liquid such as cream or egg whites vigorously with a whisk. Whisking adds air, and done for a longer period of time will make these ingredients bigger in volume.

worcestershire sauce

A savory sauce most commonly used to flavor meats, named after the town of Worcester, England, where it was first made.

yeast, active dry

Microscopic organisms known as yeasts make breads rise. They are sold as dry granules in small packets in supermarkets.

index

weldon**owen**

415 Jackson Street, Suite 200, San Francisco, CA 94111
Telephone: 415 291 0100 Fax: 415 291 8841
www.weldonowen.com

A division of
BONNIER

WILLIAMS-SONOMA, INC.
Founder and Vice-Chairman Chuck Williams

WELDON OWEN, INC.
CEO and President Terry Newell
Senior VP, International Sales Stuart Laurence
VP, Sales and Marketing Amy Kaneko
Director of Finance Mark Perrigo

VP and Publisher Hannah Rahill
Associate Publisher Amy Marr
Editorial Assistant Becky Duffet

Associate Creative Director Emma Boys
Associate Art Director Diana Heom
Junior Designer Anna Grace

Production Director Chris Hemesath
Production Manager Michelle Duggan
Color Manager Teri Bell

Text Writer Lisa Atwood
Photographer Erin Kunkel
Digital Technician Shae Rocco
Food Stylist Erin Quon
Assistant Food Stylist Victoria Woollard, Alexa Hyman
Prop Stylists Alessandra Mortola, Leigh Noe
Illustrator Salli S. Swindell

WILLIAMS-SONOMA THE COOKBOOK FOR KIDS
Conceived and produced by Weldon Owen, Inc.
In collaboration with Williams-Sonoma, Inc.
3250 Van Ness Avenue, San Francisco, CA 94109

A WELDON OWEN PRODUCTION
Copyright © 2010 Weldon Owen Inc. and Williams-Sonoma, Inc.
All rights reserved, including the right of reproduction in whole
or in part in any form.

Color separations by Embassy Graphics in Canada
Printed and bound by Toppan-Leefung Printing in
Dongguan, Guangdong Province, China

First printed in 2010
10 9 8 7 6 5
2011 2012

Library of Congress Cataloging-in-Publication data is available.

ISBN 13: 978-1-61628-018-5
ISBN 10: 1-61628-018-2

ACKNOWLEDGMENTS
Weldon Owen would like to thank the following people for their generous support in making this book:
Ken DellaPenta, Tara Duggan, Carrie Neves, Jane Tunks, and Sharron Wood.

spicy!

top pick!

sweet!

yum!

cheesy!

more please!

fruity!

party time!